Christianity
for
Buddhists

Christianity
for
Buddhists

Fredrick Farrar

The Saint Austin Press
296, Brockley Road, London, SE4 2RA
MMII

THE SAINT AUSTIN PRESS
296, Brockley Road
London, SE4 2RA

Telephone: +44 (0)20 8692 6009
Facsimile: +44 (0)20 8469 3609

Electronic mail: books@saintaustin.org
http://www.saintaustin.org

ISBN 1 901157 23 7
Copyright © Frederick Farrar, 2002.

"The right of Frederick Farrar to be identified as the author of this
work has been asserted by him in accordance with the Copyright,
Designs and Patents Act 1988."

A catalogue record for this book is available from the British Library.

Printed by Newton Printing Ltd, London, U.K.   www.newtonprinting.com

Contents

List of Illustrations

Front cover: "Christ on the Cross", Albrecht Altdorfer
(by permission of Szepmuveszeti Muzeum, Budapest)

Back cover: "San Sebastian", Alonso Berreguette
(by permission of Museo Nacional de Escultura, Valladolid)

Page 8: "Black Maha Kala", traditional Tibetan Thangka
(by permission of Mystic Buddha, www.mysticbuddha.com)

Page 24: Ouroboros

Page 31: "Wheel of Life", traditional Tibetan Thangka
(by permission of Mystic Buddha)

Page 99: "The Crucifixion", Matthias Grunewald
(by permission of The Bridgeman Art Gallery,
www.bridgeman.co.uk)

"Deep within his conscience man discovers a law which he has not laid on himself, but which he must obey."

Gaudium et Spes, document from Second Vatican Council

Typical wrathful deity of the Tibetan Buddhist tradition

Foreword

Between the years of 1990 and 1998 I trained as a lay Buddhist with teachers of the Tibetan Kagyu and Nyingma lineages. Throughout that time I meditated regularly and read copiously. At the end of it I was forty five years old.

The purpose of this small work is to answer a call that grew louder and more troubling the more I was absorbed by the Buddhist tradition. Something was wrong that I could not explain, a fact which has great significance in the chapters that follow. How did I know that something was wrong before I could articulate it in rational thought? What does this tell us about how we know right from wrong?

One day, the call came in the form of a crucifix, and that felt right - a further instance of knowing in a way that I could not explain. For me, this book gives the explanation that I didn't have then. I hope it will help others who are similarly troubled or just curious.

The presentation of Buddhist views which follows expresses my own understanding, and though I have tried to be true to my Buddhist sources it should be understood that I am no more than a participant in the disputations between different Buddhist schools. Not wishing to clutter up the main text with copious notes and references of little interest to the non-doctrinal reader, I have included an appendix in which certain possibly controversial aspects of my understanding of Buddhism, are expanded upon. I have also included an extensive bibliography to allow the reader an acquaintance with the authoritative views of the various proponents.

My concern over these issues arises from important questions expressed by a number of readers of the initial draft document. I would like to thank them for their encouragement and helpful contributions, having said which, I unequivocally take full responsibility for the views expressed within.

For their generous and, when necessary, critical readings of my work I wish to thank Professor Paul Williams of Bristol University, Fr Aidan Nichols of Blackfriars, Cambridge, Fr Roch Kereszty of the Communio Board, and my good friend Matt Osmond, an artist and lecturer working in Cornwall. Also my thanks are due to Fr Ray Gawronski, and Dr Stratford Caldecott (of Plater College, Oxford), for their helpful comments.

Lastly I must thank from the bottom of my heart the staff at St Austin Press for becoming my friends, and struggling with my many questions before finally standing with me at my reception into the Catholic Church at Easter of the first year of the third millenium of Christianity.

Hunger

I am writing this from the perspective not of the professional theologian or philosopher but of the ordinary man or woman who walks into a bookshop, is tempted to buy a book on Buddhism, and later joins a meditation group to receive instruction from a teacher. What, apart from mere curiosity, has made more and more people set out upon this by now well-trodden path?

I believe the answer to be found in the popular materialism of the mid twentieth century, which was largely the belated effect of the scientific and philosophical materialism of the nineteenth century. The popular mind at that time had not widely caught up with twentieth century science. Dazzled by the wealth of gadgetry and engineering prowess, the ordinary person was increasingly in awe of the scientist and the feeling prevailed that no human problem would not eventually be solved by science and technology. The most pressing problem of the day was who would control these twin giants of our own making. Religion seemed to many to have become redundant and was thought of as a relic from our immature past.

Materialism

But as time went by the affluent of the West soon felt dissatisfied. For one thing, the problem of political control was no easy one to solve and demanded great sacrifices. The Korean war raged in the Far East, soon to be followed by wars in Vietnam, Algeria, the Middle East, and throughout the continents of South America and Africa. In

Disillusion

the thirty or forty years after the second world war more people died in local proxy wars between the US and the USSR than had died in the world war itself. The effects of these wars on the West's moral resources were enough to take the shine off the bright new future promised by technological materialism. Great swathes of the populace became disenchanted with it, and new intellectuals soon floated to the surface of the sea of disillusionment. The result was a diverse milieu of thought, cut off from tradition and seeking every possible avenue of spiritual and moral renewal, ranging from Marxist theories of psychosocial revolution, to retreats into neo-pagan cultism. The breadth of activity was enormous and it was in this milieu that Buddhism began to grow from the rather eccentric thing that it had been amongst Western academics and itinerant mystics, to the popular phenomenon it has become today.

Spiritual resurgence

One thing that has marked this popular resurgence of spiritual hunger is a disdain for Christianity which for many crystallised whilst still in their youth. It is not surprising then that when their later spiritual interest began to awaken, they looked elsewhere than to their childhood Christianity. What is perhaps surprising is that even in their more mature years whilst they revel in the depths of philosophic and meditative inquiry offered to them by an elderly Buddhism, they continue scarcely to cast a glance at Christianity of which all they really know is their familiar but immature childhood recollection.

Naïve Christianity

I do not wish to imply that there is nothing of lasting value in the Christianity of our childhoods. Far from it - this is often just when Christianity's deepest marks are made.
But the mature rational mind requires sustenance and without it the beauty of one's first encounter with the Christian message is bound to be relegated to the same category as fairy tales and Father Christmas.

What, then, is the pulling power of Buddhism for the rational mind? It is this: that it allows the rational mind to retain its integrity right up until the moment that it arrives at its own inherent limit and looks in awe upon the impenetrable mystery beyond itself from which it derives its own existence. Only this unfathomable mystery can satisfy the spiritual hunger of mankind, and Buddhism performs admirably well as one of the worlds great natural religions in allowing man to appreciate it.

Buddhism's attraction

Power by Reduction

Classical scientific materialism tries to understand the world by analysing things into smaller, simpler parts ending up at the atoms of physical matter. By formulating the physical laws which evidently govern the behaviour of these parts, and then recombining them, the materialistic scientist hopes to understand the behaviour of the more complex whole. At the same time his theoretical method is a perfect metaphor for the practical method of modern industry which breaks nature up into raw materials in order to recombine them in the form of new commodities and technologies.

Reductive materialism

While this methodology has proved to be a very successful tool in the scientist's repertoire, it has also been shown to be very limited. For one thing, the whole is more than the sum of its parts. At a given level of complexity wholly new behaviours arise which are specific to that level and cannot be understood without reference to the interdependence of things at that level. Thus, whereas in the beginning physics was seen as the fundamental ground of all science, later the sciences of relationship such as cybernetics, psychology and ecology came to the fore. Indeed, physics itself was reformed with Einstein's discovery that space and time are not independent absolutes but form a unity in which each is related to the other in a quite precise way. It was no longer possible to make an absolute distinction between matter and energy. At the same time a number of his contemporaries were

Relativism

discovering that not only was the atom not the smallest possible particle of matter, it was not very simple either.

Environmental exhaustion By the early years of the twentieth century science had been revolutionised and the way was open for the new sciences to flower. It was not until the nineteen sixties, however, that the message began to properly sink in. By then the habit of exploiting nature by reducing it to raw materials and recombining them in ways which satisfied man's rapacious appetite for novelty and technical mastery, was showing signs of having finally begun to squeeze nature past the limit of its powers of regeneration. Near the end of the sixties the first mathematical models were worked out which showed that the rate of consumption of raw materials was rising exponentially and could not be sustained. Already, forty years ahead of the first concrete evidence of the event, scientists predicted global warming as a result of burning greenhouse gases. The people who had least to gain from the inertia of the established political economy, and who responded to these messages most passionately, were the young and the world's dispossessed, a fact which led to volatile times and an air even of revolution.

Discovering the East The sixties were full of fervour for both the new and the ancient, and in that fervour people turned to the East for spiritual example. The East's emphasis upon individual karma or action as the cause of this world's beautiful array of evolving systems and species, struck a chord with those involved in the modern sciences, as well as in the more traditional arts. In contrast, they associated the Old Testament's proclamation that man was created to have dominion over the earth, with that practise of ruthless exploitation which they now saw as the enemy of life. Having gotten a common enemy in their sights many social movements now began to come together. The civil rights movement which at first fought for black people against racial prejudice soon took up the cause of women's oppression by men, and not long after that took up the cause of homosexuals' oppression by heterosexuals. The common bond between these movements was repression by established authority at every level of society. And out of this bond a new collective identity was emerging which soon would be propagated to a new generation who would have no direct knowledge of its origins and roots. It is to this identity that Buddhism has its greatest appeal.

The post-modern identity

It is my belief that the movement begun in the nineteen sixties against the reductive materialism of the previous hundred and fifty years, was a vital step in the spiritual regeneration of the Christian West, but that that movement was deflected into the blind alley of a new *spiritual* reductionism, perhaps the most subtle example of which is Buddhism.

Spiritual reductionism

What are the most general outlines of this spiritual reductionism? Well, whereas materialism reduced natural things to primary components or raw materials, spiritual reductionism reduces natural things to pure spiritual energy. And almost always the motive is similar to that of materialism: to gain power over natural things and above all over oneself and one's vulnerability to suffering.

Power over suffering

In fact spiritual reductionism has been one of humanity's vices for far longer than materialism. The latter's predominance arose only when the bonded labour of feudalism was transformed into the free labour of capitalism. Then became general the perception of life as an abstract power available for purchase by the capitalist, to be used by him in a manner best organised to yield profit. But long before capitalism, long before medieval feudalism, long before Christianity and long before Judaism, spiritual reductionism in the form of magic was the predominant form of spirituality practised by mankind. It was this practise, seen by the Jews as an aberration, a blasphemous disobedience to the one true God, that Judaism and Christianity unequivocally rejected. The Judaeo-Christian tradition understands all natural things to have been created, each according to their own kind, by God. All, including man, behave according to their God-given natures. In the case of animals this means that they all behave according to their instincts. But in the case of man, he was given free will and so was forced to choose between obeying God's will or deciding what to do for himself. For a while he obeyed God's will and lived in paradise. But eventually, tempted by the serpent, he took power unto himself and denied the authority of God. For that act of selfish arrogance he was cast out of paradise and forced to suffer the hardships of an ordinary life.

What this teaching tells us is that there is a proper God-given way for we human beings to live, a way which corresponds perfectly to our created natures. It is precisely this teaching that both the spiritual and materialistic forms of reductionism reject. For them, man's created nature can be reduced to some sort of element which can be manipulated by the will in order to gain power. In each case this is a mutilation of man's proper nature and a denial of the will of the Creator.

Since modern people commonly do not believe in the *Neo-paganism* existence of a Divine Creator it is only natural that their first spiritual yearnings will lead them to perceive the sacred as an impersonal element which empowers the world that they understand. And since they are a part of that empowered world and being human have free will, how can they fail to entertain the thought that they might conceivably be able to wield power over the sacred element? That is what all magic seeks to achieve and is the reason it is seen as repugnant by those who believe in the personal authority of the Creator God . In short, to the Jew *Coveting God's* or the Christian, the magician seeks to manipulate God, *power* and no greater blasphemy can be imagined.

Let us pause for thought now for we are far ahead of the *Buddhism as* average secular mind which doesn't believe in any form of *proof of the* sacredness whatever. Apart from direct revelation, which *sacred* the modern sceptical mind would probably not accept no matter how convincing it may appear, how can we come to a sure belief in the sacred? It is just here that in Buddhism lies its greatest value and strength. Like a razor-sharp sword - the sword of Manjushri - it cuts through the apparent solidity of our perceptions of the world until ultimately it seems so transparent that we no longer see the multitude of things as separate but as different aspects of one inconceivable being.

How does Buddhism achieve this transparency of perception and why? It does so by arduous systematic training involving different forms of meditation practise in order to find freedom from suffering. According to tradition, the Buddha - Siddhartha Gotama - was a prince of the Shakya tribe which lived in Northern India around 500BC. He was a very gifted boy clearly destined for greatness, and his father, who doted on him, tried to protect him from the pains and distractions of the world whilst steering him towards kingship. Siddhartha excelled in all aspects of his education, from the martial arts to the more intellectual forms of knowledge. On his coming of age he was happily married to a beautiful wife who soon bore their child. He had everything that worldly life could offer and yet he soon realised that he lacked for something. He sensed that this happy life he was living had been contrived by his father and that his knowledge of real life was correspondingly limited. Driven by this sense of inadequacy he arranged for his servant to take him out of the royal compound into the world beyond. It was then that he saw at first hand the four types of suffering undergone by all sentient beings - birth, ageing, sickness and death. Seeing these he was overcome by a grief so intense he could hardly bear it. Filled with compassion for the suffering beings he saw all around him he vowed there and then not to rest until he had found a way which all might follow, of attaining liberation from suffering. He returned to his father and announced that he was entering into the religious life, whereupon he began a seven year sojourn in the meditative life as a forest dweller. During that period he studied under the greatest teachers known at the time, but at the end of it all, severely emaciated from extreme ascetic practises, he concluded that theirs was not the way to liberation from suffering. Turning away from them he first of all attended to the needs of his body. He obtained food from a kind passer-by and washed himself in a nearby pool. Then, sitting beneath a Pipal tree by the water's side, he decided not to move on until he had attained enlightenment. He entered into a deep meditation and by the next morning had attained what he had long searched for.

The Pali Canon, generally regarded as representing the earliest form of Buddhism, cites clinging to things at face value as what the Buddha took to be the principal source of our suffering. "The uninformed person," says the Buddha in one of the sutras [1], "sees solidity as solidity, and having done so thinks of solidity with reference to solidity, from the standpoint of solidity and thinks: 'solidity is mine'." He sees things in this way, says the *Defectiveness of* Buddha, because he does not properly understand reality. *ordinary* The Buddha invites us to look closely at how things come *understanding* to be and directs us to the fact that all things are the results *Dependent* of causes and conditions. When this seemingly simple fact *origination* is properly understood it becomes clear that since everything is constantly arising and passing away nothing can be seen solely in reference to itself. The Buddhist tradition has formalised this insight referring to it as 'emptiness of self'. Without a permanent self, asks the *Non-self* Buddha, what is there to cling to or call one's own? All things, whether traditionally thought of as inner or outer from a personal point of view, appear as a result of preceding causes and conditions. We know that we are able to intend our own actions and so we know that we have a personal existence - the Buddha affirms this in the sutras - but when we encounter our bodies and become familiar with worldly things we come to see ourselves and

Dependence of the finite on the infinite the world as finite. We lose sight of that endless flow of one thing into another which makes the finite world possible. We forget that things are only transient states in a sea of change. Realising that our bodies continue to grow and express our intentions we naturally come to identify ourselves with our bodies. We feel that we are

Clinging to the finite they. But, lacking wisdom, when we feel this we ensnare ourselves in our ignorance of the fluid aspect of our nature and cling desperately instead to what we perceive as the finiteness of our worldly life. Once we have done this our sufferings inevitably accumulate and compound upon each other as reality proceeds to thwart our every wish and overwhelm us with every kind of physical and emotional pain. In addition our self-clinging has become a self-replicating cause whose results, the Buddha believed, extend our personal stream of existence beyond our death, giving rise to rebirth as yet another suffering being in a further life-cycle. Thus he explained the endless round of suffering in conditioned existence or Samsara.

Liberation as non-attachment The Buddha taught that we should recognise the impermanence at the heart of our lives and embrace it fully. In properly understanding and accepting impermanence the wise person could learn the art of non-attachment and allow unhealthy passions such as greed or hatred to be subdued. With this the cause of rebirth would be removed and suffering would come to an end. In the Buddha's own quest for truth the deepening of this insight culminated, on the evening of his enlightenment, in an

22

acute crisis of identity symbolised by the temptations and terrors which the demon Mara put in his way. Eventually Mara was overcome and the Buddha's instinctive identification with self-permanence collapsed leaving a very different experience of reality from that which preceded it. He described this new experience as peace, compassion, non-attachment, liberation, truth, enlightenment, non-suffering, attainment of the world of Brahma or Nirvana, and having done what had to be done, he expected, with the dissolution of his body, never to return to this world again.

Nirvana

From a philosophical point of view the Buddha's teaching provides a valuable and accessible introduction to the mysteries of existence which lie right beneath our noses. In pointing out that things arose only within a continuum of causes and effects he revealed something profound and strange at the very heart of our everyday beliefs. Everything that gives a thing its particular thingness lies in the realm of past causes. But past causes do not exist *now*. Therefore a thing's present existence, though the manner of its manifestation has been conditioned by past states, cannot right now be *caused* by them. Present existence cannot but have some self-existent source which gives it its reality. This the Buddha called the *unconditioned* since in itself it does not depend upon causes or conditions. The Buddha deliberately avoided saying that the continuum of causes and effects consisted of matter or spirit or mind or

The unconditioned

The Buddha's silence

23

The Uroboros

The ancient image of the Uroboros, which can be found all over the world, symbolises the mystery of self-regeneration. The community of living beings, in competition with each other for survival, are represented by the visible body of the serpent. In that competition, sooner or later, all will lose their lives and become food for others. These are represented by that part of the serpent's body which it is consuming and incorporating into its future body. Traditionally, the ordinary snake shedding its skin, and the moon waxing and waning as it progresses through its monthly cycle, are also used as symbols for this self-substantiating aspect of reality.

any other underlying substance^2. He knew very well that any attempt to define the present reality in its true essence was an impossibility and bound to mislead those who had not yet understood. The present moment, that is, the moment of presenting being, has no temporal dimensions. Viewed chronologically, it is no more than a moving point within a stream of change. To say that things are part of a continuum is to recognise the unity of all things in a single indivisible reality whose eternally enduring nature contains and creates all the phenomena of space and time. The past is remembered as the determinate or finite state of the present. It exists only in the present. The future is the range of potential states open to the present. It also exists only in the present. Thus, by the eternal endurance of its invisible source the visible present pours itself out into a particular future, and in so doing determines a new past and a new future potential.

Eternal presence

In trying to understand this continuum of causes and conditions we have to get away from thinking of it as a linear chain existing in some sort of space. For to be a universal description of reality, the continuum has to include everything. The continuum is both figure and ground. It includes the space in which things happen. Suddenly we are looking into the mouth of the Uroboros, the mythical snake eating its own tail alluded to in the form of the serpentine tempter in the biblical story of man's fall. Its present existence receives its future substance by consuming itself, apparently a form of substantiation determined by the feeding relationships

The uroboric vision

between present entities. In this uroboric view of reality the end of one self is the beginning of others. The Uroboros is Samsara - the eternal round of suffering. In this reality, the lifespan of an entity is the duration of its memory. It re-members itself by consuming others. When it can no longer re-member itself, its members fall apart and *it* ceases to exist. Its existence is then consumed by others so that they can exist. When an entity re-members itself its members are affected by others. It continually incorporates these effects among its members, so that change is translated into the compound structure of its body. The structure of its body, then, contains an analogue of the changes it has been subjected to, which appears as a being in a world. We call this appearance "experience". When our re-membering ends, both our body and our mind cease to exist.

The Uroboros is an enigmatic symbol. Its value lies in helping to understand how things change and grow. This is the sphere of causation. But in showing how they are *caused* it tends, in an equation of form and being, to obscure how they *exist*. In the Uroboros, when the tail is consumed, it appears to give renewed existence to the body, which in the concrete case indicates that in death a thing releases its being to others. But as we saw earlier, although a thing's form is caused by prior conditions its present actuality is a fact entirely free of them since they cannot be explained by ordinary causality. Also, given that its form, namely that which gives it its phenomenal character, *is* a product of causality, neither can we conclude that the thing possesses a self-existent actuality. The only conclusion we can come to is that the uncaused actuality of the thing's presence is not its possession but its *source*. That being the case, there are only two possibilities as to how this source realises things: substantiation, or creation. The spiritualist and materialist *Substantiation* forms of reductionism discussed earlier both opt for substantiation, the theistic traditions for creation. When the source does no more than manifest its existence in the form of phenomenal objects while they themselves carry out all of the actions which cause the universe to grow and diversify, then it is seen as no more than a substance, albeit an ineffable one. When, on the other hand, it is seen *Creation* to will things' existence, both in substance and in form, then it is seen as a creator. When that is one's view, the Uroboros itself comes to be seen as "that most subtle of God's creations" spoken of in the bible. The serpentine view, in challenging God's authorship of his creations, blinds primordial man and all men since, to its own creatureliness and the arrogance of its divine pretensions. In so doing it tempts man to an equally arrogant and *Temptation* lustful ignorance which separates him from God.

Some Buddhists [3] believe that when the mind is present in its absolute immediacy, appearing as first this and then that it is in fact pure unconditioned essence. This unconditioned essence which has the power to appear as ourselves and the world we inhabit is known by them as Buddha Nature. It is always empty of anything other than *Buddha Nature* itself, and is the true nature of all things, whether apparently inner or outer. An indication of the subtlety of this view is that it can quite easily accommodate the notion of a non-conceptual experience of conceptuality. This is because it believes that openness, clarity and sensitivity - the qualities of mind which seem to display illusory experience - are themselves aspects of Absolute Reality which are knowable in illusory experience. Thus their renunciation of conceptuality does not involve trying to eliminate all conceptuality from experience. Rather, it

Going beyond conceptuality

means going *beyond* the conceptuality of ordinary experience to that reality within it which is not conceptual. The analogy is frequently used of a mirror in which the

The cosmic mirror

image retains all its particular characteristics whilst at the same time belonging to the reflective properties of the mirror. Here the Absolute is likened to the mirror and the world to the image it reflects. From the Judaeo-Christian perspective there is here a more or less conscious identification of our own essence with God, which only repeats man's original sin. The effect of this is subtle however, for this tradition does not try to *suicidally* dissolve the many into the Absolute One. Rather, there arises a fundamental identification with the One which sees the limitations of one's life as belonging to the plenitude of its facets. As such they are allowed to run their natural course, but without emotional identification or attachment. To facilitate this way of being the living of

Life as offering to Buddha

one's life is liturgically offered to the Buddha as part of one's routine devotional practise, and where deep emotions are allowed expression, as in Tibetan Vajrayana or tantric Buddhism, these emotions are transformed into servants of Absolute Reality.

Other Buddhists [4] refute this view seeing in it a superficial understanding of self-emptiness. They insist that even the most apparently immediate and elementary of perceptions, seeing a colour for instance, depends upon our eye and brain remembering a period of contact of sufficient duration to convey the wave dimensions of light which correspond to the experience of that particular colour. In other words, even our experience of the immediate present is already a meaningful memory, an act of understanding from which, I would argue, it is impossible to extract the intellect or conceptuality. A colour is, from the moment we perceive it, a concept ready and available to the intellect. The notion of non-conceptual experience of phenomena, is, for me, deeply confusing and misleading. The present as such can never be immediately experienced as an object of knowledge. Immediate experience is always the experience of meaningful memory compounded over a period of time. It seems to be the present reality but it is not. Though we experience it *in* the present it is never an experience *of* the present. Quite simply: beyond conceptuality, although there must be unconscious awareness waiting in readiness to take hold of significant new events, there is no mind. Awareness, with or without conscious content, belongs to the continuum of causes and effects. It is not the substance of that continuum. The qualities and measure of *all* experiences are always the results of prior causes and conditions,

The remembered present

including the sense that they are appearing to and within our minds. Openness, clarity and sensitivity therefore, are aspects of perception. They arise in continuity with their causes and conditions and are not, as such, perceptible aspects of the Absolute.

The Absolute transcends all ordinary experience

Parallel with Catholic scholasticism

In respecting both the limits and mystery of finite knowledge the Buddha mirrored the concerns of Greek philosophy as well as anticipating important elements in the theology of the Catholic saint Thomas Aquinas. Aquinas, without necessarily knowing it, recapitulated many of the Buddha's arguments with regard to conditioned existence and finite knowledge. His thought, though leading to the certainty of God's existence, made it clear that the infinity of God's nature cannot be perceived by the finite mind. The hidden God of the Judaeo-Christian tradition is necessarily hidden in his own infinity.

Distinction between emanation and incarnation

Although there may appear to be a similarity in the Buddhist idea of the Absolute appearing as the things of this world and the Christian belief that God appeared within this world in the person of Jesus of Nazareth, a deeper understanding of Christian theology shows that this similarity is superficial. For Christ is recognised as the incarnation, the finite embodiment, of the Word of God, the Logos, the divine creative person who forms things in their particular uniqueness. This act of self-embodiment by the Word is not the same as his creation of worldly things. Buddha Nature thinkers conceal this distinction

The Wheel of Life

The Buddhist Wheel of Life symbolises the chain of interdependent origination. Its uroboric nature is self-evident. The segments within the wheel represent the different realms of existence recognised by Buddhist cosmology - gods, jealous gods, humans, animals, hungry ghosts and hell beings. Together they constitute Samsara - the eternal round of suffering - being devoured in the painting by Mara, the Lord of Death. Rebirth into one or another of these realms according to the character of one's accumulated karma, is inevitable as long as one remains trapped within the wheel. One's only hope is liberation through enlightenment, and to facilitate this a Buddha is present in every segment.

with their notion of the Absolute appearing as non-conceptual mind. In this way of thinking, worldly things are no more than emanations or embodiments of the Absolute, which in essence makes them all divine. Salvation then appears to lie in recognising the divine nature of ordinary existence. This trend within Buddhism which, in its identification with the Absolute and its recognition of true spontaneity is pantheistic, does not reflect the Buddha's teaching in the Pali Canon. Though for him the potential for action lay within the unconditioned, and though the first experience of self could only have arisen spontaneously within it, whatever could be experienced could not be the unconditioned as such but only spontaneous self-clinging which began the chain of karma resulting in the world we all experience. He demonstrated with relentless persistence the emptiness or non-self-existence of all appearances of any kind and saw salvation as lying exclusively in knowledge of this self-emptiness which *pointed* towards the unconditioned. In doing so he brought his disciples to the very brink of an understanding of divine creativity[5]. Beyond that he abstained from speaking of it, not out of absolute agnosticism on his part as some commentators have suggested, but because his manner of knowing it did not depend on, nor could be expressed in positive terms.

Karmic formation   The Buddha's understanding of self-emptiness only achieves its full significance in the light of his understanding of how sentient beings come into existence, and it is here that I believe the principal weakness of

Buddhism lies. He believed that self-clinging, a form of action or karma, resulted in the arising of future living entities whose conditioned nature doomed them to suffer the pains of life. He believed that the solution to suffering lay in cutting the chain of causes and conditions giving rise to conditioned existence. And this is where realisation of self-emptiness came in. It acted as a cause-ending cause. It was the knife which cut the chain, resulting at first in rendering the suffering of one's present life transparent, and subsequently in ending one's particular stream of conditioned existence. Not being reborn, one's personal stream of existence would end in nirvana, peace, non-suffering, that unconditioned reality from which our self-clinging must have come in the beginning. It is just here where I think Buddhism betrays us. I do not believe that life is the result of ignorant self-clinging and I do not believe that so-called "wisdom" has the right to manipulate life in the way that I think in Buddhism it does. One sees this manipulation in early Buddhism's general renunciation of worldly involvements, particularly of marriage, and in later periods in the moral as well as physical fearlessness of the compassionate bodhisattva. Ultimately this fearlessness is different to that of the Western hero. For the Western hero's self-sacrifice is necessarily tragic due to his unquestioned love of self. He fearlessly plunges himself into suffering because his love of others transcends his love for his own self. The bodhisattva, in contrast, goes beyond fear precisely in order to go beyond the suffering self to that unconditioned peace which all Buddhists strive to attain. His wish for others is that they may attain it too. In both Vajrayana and Zen the bodhisattva's teacher will often flout the norms of conventional morality in an attempt to reveal the non-duality of what he believes to be the Absolute essence. No more evidence is needed to show how Buddhism, even when it rejects any idea that the Absolute can be the object of finite experience, still tries to identify with the Absolute rather than conform to its creative will.

Equanimity as indifference

Depending upon the particular variant, Buddhism may be seen as either monistic or pantheistic, not because of any explicit assertions by the Buddha of a spiritual substance in things, but because his understanding of the karmic origins of things subtly implies it. It leaves God with nothing to do but unite things as one being, a unity which many of the later schools of Buddhism mistake for Absolute Reality itself. Whether the unconditioned is thought of as primal chaos from which the universe emerges by chance, or whether it be thought of as a primordial ground in which the eternal principles of existence lie immanent, such a view must surely lend a tone of ultimate arbitrariness to worldly existence. For in each view, though it does not shun the world, neither does it properly value it. Worldly existence is suffering, something one wishes release from. That wish is at the core of its moral system. The Buddha's equanimity and compassion for others are motivated by his search for liberation from suffering. For the Christian his equanimity is indistinguishable from indifference since it fails to appreciate the divinely ordained propriety of worldly existence. For him human existence is valued for the karmic opportunity it provides to finally liberate oneself from suffering. It is not valued for its humanness as such.

In trying to render an account of Buddhism which allows the reader to understand the *meaning* of its practise I have so far neglected the practise itself. To avoid the Christian reader being misled and the Buddhist feeling understandably aggrieved, it is necessary to rectify this neglect. It seems inevitable that in trying to demonstrate Buddhism's differences from Christianity the humaneness it does express is obscured through oversimplification. The Christian reader who has had no acquaintance with Buddhists may come away with the impression that they are entirely distant and aloof. This would be an unfair exaggeration and is not the case. To avoid that impression it is necessary to become more familiar with the Buddhist practise of non-attachment.

Buddhism in practise

Non-attachment is realised not through turning one's back on experience but by radically accepting it. The impermanence of things which on first consideration may seem a gloomy aspect to focus on, becomes so pervasive in the meditator's experience that the very character of experience changes. For whereas in the beginning impermanence may be thought of as a slice of existence sandwiched between an infinite past and an infinite future, as direct experience of it deepens it is no longer experienced as the *loss* of things which once existed, but

Buddhist aloofness?

Non-attachment as acceptance of continuity

as the *continuity* of a reality in which permanent things do not exist and never have.

Vividness of non-attachment What is happening here is that reality is beginning to be perceived with vivid clarity, perhaps for the first time since the meditator was a small child. Maturity alas, has the tendency to bring with it a growing film of familiarity which obscures our immediate perception of reality. We come to see what we expect to see and ignore what we are not expecting. We attach our perceptions and feelings to our preconceived ideas as if the characteristics of those ideas were characteristics of reality itself. Thus, when we look at an apple for instance, our first perception of it brings to mind our idea of an apple, after which we are apt to see our idea rather than the actual apple. We do this with all things, including ourselves. In our own case, when we experience things, our first perception brings to mind our idea of ourself and again we begin to experience the idea rather than our actual self. The Buddhist practise of mindfulness works against this tendency. It does so not by trying to eradicate ideas but by loosening our fixation on them and opening ourselves to new experience. This is achieved by seeing reality more clearly so that the confusion between the two is removed.

With regard to our self-image, the nearest Western term for this is "ego", that identity which one treasures so much but which is actually no more than one's accumulated memories of one's life. This is the self we initially believe to be the owner of all our experience and which orders it according to its own familiar character. It is an important, indispensable structure in our mind but it is only a structure whose validity is dependent upon our keeping in touch with reality. Along with this clarification of experience, certain emotions such as delight in natural movement, or in novelty, are enhanced, while others such as churlishness or a sense of insult when reality doesn't match our expectations of it, are lost.

There has been no attempt here to eliminate the ego outright, only a determination to purify it of what are thought to be conceptual distortions by seeing it clearly for what it is and opening it to otherness. When the meditator reaches out beyond ego he is simply reaching out to reality. He recognises the ego as a participant in his experience not an owner outside of it. There invariably awaits for him many an experience of wry humour as he confronts the ego's natural tendency towards pomposity and self- aggrandisement.

Non-attachment as going beyond ego

The investigation does not end here however. For once clear seeing becomes established, a new more profound emptiness begins to be noticed. The more the meditator focuses on present awareness the more the fabricatedness of things begins to unfold, and in the traditions which most closely follow the Buddha's own meditation practise as it is described in the Pali Canon, meditative absorption results in a state of luminous awakeness in which all ordinary perceptions cease. This state is said to be filled with a boundless compassion which has no referential

Going beyond egolessness

object. How the Buddha understood this experience is key to our grasp of what Buddhism does. He took it to mean

Self-emptiness

that experience is empty not only of conceptual overlays such as the ego, but of its very self-existence. In the actuality of the present nothing is perceived since the conditions giving rise to things' existence have no place there. This luminous experience of the mind unconditioned by any ordinary object was a tremendous discovery for the Buddha but he was under no illusion that liberation from suffering consisted in remaining in such a state. For a being whose body would continue to arise due to past karma, remaining in such a state would be no more than a contrivance. The true significance of his discovery

Liberation as path of karma-ending karma

was the certain knowledge that liberation from suffering was only attained by way of the path of karma-ending karma or non-clinging. Thus the enlightened person lived for the remainder of his life without attachment.

The path of karma-ending karma consisted in two aspects: the practise of meditation which gave one the certainty of things' self-emptiness; and the path of discipline which involved a careful balance between acknowledging the necessary ways in which one is entwined with one's world, and renunciation of thirst for unnecessary, conditioned, or, what is the same thing, contingent existence. Clearly this involved a basic sense of morality for to acknowledge one's necessary involvements with others meant acknowledging their necessary involvements with each other. Buddhist morality was therefore based on a clear recognition of things' interdependence and consisted in honouring other's needs. This included the *Enjoyment* many delightful experiences which life naturally offers as well as its many stings, but beyond what was karmically necessary, the Buddhist path demanded renunciation if *The morality of* rebirth and further suffering was to be avoided. The *renunciation* resulting ethic was a quite beautiful but rather frugal one with regard to creatureliness, avoiding as it did sexuality and worldliness. In this avoidance we can see an undermining of the natural sense of creaturely propriety. For a person behaving naturally never restricts his worldly life to the merely necessary but rather pursues the perfect and the beautiful. The Buddhist's meditative awareness, cultivated as his primary means of cutting through confusion, goes beyond merely putting the ego back in touch with reality. It tries to rise above suffering, or more accurately perhaps, to get behind it, by interrupting the aesthetic formation of worldly feelings and meanings. In seeking to perfect his realisation of selflessness or non-dual Buddha Nature, which is not a vacant emptiness but an absolute fullness of being in which suffering has no place, he becomes unable to perfect his human creatureliness in which suffering is of the utmost value.

Some later traditions of Buddhism[6], influenced by the *Enlightened* "mind-only" school of thought believed that realisation of *existence* emptiness consisted in experiencing ordinary reality without dualistic distinctions. Enlightened existence involved seeing things as emanations of the Absolute, rather than as conditioned entities. In those schools, the passions which for earlier Buddhists were seen as poisons leading to rebirth, were now believed to have enlightened expressions as well as poisonous ones. In these traditions, which have a distinctly alchemical character, there developed, as well as meditation on formless emptiness, numerous meditations which encouraged seeing ordinary existence as non-duality or Oneness. By recognising their wrathful energies as its manifestations, even demons could be transformed into agents of Buddha Nature, serving as protectors of the truth and the path to enlightenment. The meditator in these schools realises non-attachment when his will flows naturally within and from out of, non-duality. The *urgency* of his will arises from specific conditions affecting his body. The particular *expression* of his will arises from decisions which themselves are conditioned by his previous thoughts and attitudes. When those thoughts and attitudes include the belief that all things exist only in dependence on causes and conditions, he no longer clings to the converse belief that either he or the objects of his desire, exist in and of themselves. Without this clinging and attachment, even though he has a body with all its feelings and sensitivity, he remains, as the Buddha describes it, *unborn*. And being unborn, though there is suffering, he does not suffer. This, I think, is the equivalent of what the Buddha called "liberation with remainder", as opposed to final liberation "without remainder" which ensued after the enlightened person's body had passed away.

Grace and poise

To accomplish this he must come to know nature intimately and perfect his essential grace and poise. It as if he were learning to dance with the world, unhindered by craving, like a baby's for its lost womb, or by clinging to selfish ambitions which cut him off from others. His path possesses great beauty and has much to recommend it, but it is disputed by many Buddhists who believe its view of emptiness to be superficial. For them it mistakes self-emptiness for egolessness and thus fails to penetrate the full depth of the mystery which the Buddha revealed[7]. This is not to deny the value of the attainment of egolessness, only to say that self-emptiness means very much more than that. This distinction has considerable significance for the Christian tradition since it is only when self-emptiness is understood as being beyond all phenomenal experience that it points beyond monism or pantheism to the Judaeo-Christian understanding of the creator God. Also, as with all other later developments of Buddhism, it continues to be marred by the Buddha's understanding of ignorant self-clinging as the root cause of conditioned existence. The problem is not that even in the midst of intense passion the enlightened person dwells always in a stillness *void* of passion, for all who forget themselves in the battle of life dwell momentarily in this empty centre. The problem is that he goes too far with it. By removing the concept of self from the chain of causation, all of the emotions which would result from the sense of one's being an inherent subject no longer arise. To me this seems to involve an effort to subtly eradicate the fullness of subjectivity, so that one is presented with the anomaly of immense existential presence yet strangely little *emotional* colour and depth, a combination which adversely affects the conscience. Subject and object are seen merely as interdependents in the continuity of being. Subjective feelings and acts are seen to arise in dependence on contacts with others in conjunction with prior emotional attitudes and preconceptions. When both subject and object are understood as results of earlier actions, self as either subject or object is seen to be no more than an illusion, a conceptual or perceptual construct. In the wake of this understanding the self is realised as unconditioned peace. But in pursuing this peace the Buddha's thought transgresses the bounds which are proper to our kind and diminishes our human value. Though his path may lead to great acts of compassion, it is a compassion deluded by a spurious understanding of self. It is a misunderstanding resulting from a profound but erroneous belief that the reality of things must consist in their being the illusory appearance of a substantially real essence. In this way of thinking the essence and the illusory appearance are identical, the problem being that the human mind is taken in by the appearance and identifies with part of it as its own. The Christian, in contrast, would say that this self-identification by the animal intelligence with what it takes to be its own part of reality, is not a problem at all but perfectly appropriate, as also are the natural emotions associated with it. To not take up this part of reality as one's own is, to the Christian, an intellectual and emotional rejection of God's gift of existence, a rejection which strips existence of its proper subjective meaning.

Loss of humanity?

Rejection of the gift of existence

42

Man's God-given task with regard to the natural world is to perfect his exercise of his monarchical dominion over it in accordance with God's will. His task is not to limit his self-interest to the merely necessary in a false identification of his essence with the Absolute or God. Any such identification which purports to unite the individual with the Divine or Absolute, merely reduces the person's emotional commitment to his own unique existence. Suffering is accepted but no one suffers, which is no acceptance of suffering at all. There is only a suppression of the aesthetic faculty in its creaturely context, a suppression which transforms worldly feeling or desire into mere sensation. Suffering is not endured sacrificially by one who loves his created life enough to know his proper place in the world, but rather is neutralised by an intellectual manipulation of the emotions which denies a *significant* distinction between self and others.

Suffering without a sufferer

What is important to grasp here is that for the Christian, Buddhism's moral character is compromised by its belief that ordinary existence results from ignorant self-clinging. It is this belief which leads mainstream Buddhists to renounce the fullness of worldly life, and tantric Buddhists to go to excess. In respect of Buddhism's overcoming of selfish egocentricity it has much to offer the Judaeo-Christian tradition. But with regard to the deeper levels of existence, the biblical traditions view life as the result not of *ignorant* self-clinging but of *inspired* self-clinging, and in so thinking they affirm not only the karmic necessity of

Inspired self-clinging

natural existence but also the beauty of its perfection. The simple truth is that if one loves nature one accepts its propriety. One accepts nature not just passively but as a rightful fact which not only happens to *be* but which, more importantly, *should* be. What allows us to appreciate this essentially moral aspect of reality is our aesthetic faculty. It so happens that we human beings are endowed with precisely the type of knowledge necessary to compensate for our lack of animal instincts. At the same time as we left behind our instincts and overcame the limitations of every particular place in nature, we enhanced our ability to

Knowledge as appreciation of beauty appreciate beauty, which allowed us to understand the value of those limitations. Though free from any particular place in nature, our sense of beauty could tell us that we depend upon the harmony of all nature. We understand nature first and foremost not by way of instinct nor by arid analytical intellect but by our ability to appreciate beauty,

Self-perfection an appreciation which urges us to perfect both our world and ourselves in its beautifying light.

Reduction as immorality I do not believe that the methods of reducing reality to either spirit - as the magical traditions do - or to matter - as the modern scientific tradition has done - can be reconciled with love for life. At its root, the question of the difference between pantheistic emanation and monotheistic creation is not a technical or intellectual one - it is a moral one. Only a view which recognises the integrity of living entities can be considered to truly appreciate life, and it is only the aesthetic appreciation of life, not the logic or erudition of the intellect, that can be a proper criterion for evaluating such a view. At bottom, the notion of monotheistic creation triumphs over monistic and pantheistic emanation simply because it is more beautiful, more perfect, more loving.

The beauty of monotheism

The Abrahamic traditions, believing as they do in a creator God responsible for the existence of all things, do appreciate life in a way which Buddhism, poised between magic and science, does not. Furthermore, the notion of divine creation solves many of the problems which Buddhist thinkers have grappled with for centuries. Some Buddhists show with great rigor how all things and all perceptions of things can only exist dependently, a view which rules out any immediate appearance of the Absolute. Yet others rightly recognise that Absolute Being must in some way account for the world we experience. It seems to me that the notion of creation resolves the difference between these two schools of thought. In this notion, living beings are understood to be created from nothing by God - that Absolute Being whose very nature is to exist. Creation from nothing by a necessarily existent being explains both self-emptiness and the true connection between Absolute reality and conditioned existence. According to Christian theology, when God wills a thing to exist, it comes into existence and has its being *in* God. From the moment of its creation God continues to hold it in existence. In this view, a thing's existence is fundamentally *given* by God. It is only the result of its own self-clinging to the extent that God created self-clinging as part of its nature. That self-clinging, as distinct

Self-emptiness as sign of creation from nothing

45

from ego-clinging, is meant to be there and is inspired by God's will.

Rejection of emanationism

I think this is a far better description and understanding of the facts that we know than any couched in terms of emanation or manifestation of Absolute nature. What these leave out is the gift of creation coming from God, a view which clearly affirms the difference between the creature and the Creator. The Absolute intended and still intends us to be particular human beings with a large measure of free will. This demands the perfection on our part of our human creatureliness, not realisation of what we mistakenly believe to be our divine essence. Unlikely as it may seem, our biggest problem remains our disobedience to divine will, just as the bible sets out at its very beginning in the book of Genesis.

Perfection as creatureliness

The Buddha image and the image of Christ

Two images in particular sum up for me the weakness of Buddhism and the strength of Christianity. One is the image of a wrathful Buddha, adorned with body parts, draped in flayed human and animal skin, his eyes utterly implacable and unperturbed by the raw ferocity of existence. The other is the image of Jesus Christ, his body pierced and broken on a crude wooden cross, whose willing acceptance of such a torment of physical pain and human rejection does not spare him the ultimate despair expressed when he cries out, "My God, my God, why hast thou forsaken me?!" In the Buddhist Thangka painting the central figure depicts the indestructibility of what is thought to be our essential nature. The result is terrifying

46

in its indifference to pain and horror. In contrast, in Christ's agony on the cross, though there is much to be horrified by, we encounter no indifference. On the contrary, we are called to accept the horror as it is. Here, suffering far from being alleviated by the renunciation of opinions about it, is felt with all the intensity of the natural emotions. Suffering is suffered wholeheartedly with all of the aversion proper to it. It is not manipulated in any way. Indeed in the depths of Christian tradition suffering is seen as a divine punishment for original sin. It is meant to be punishing, and to try to strip it of its naturally abhorrent value is seen as an additional personal sin. What Jesus showed us is that we must accept living and dying in obedience to God without seeking to compromise the vulnerability of our created nature.

Compromising Creatureliness

I suggested at the outset that Buddhism was playing a central role in the formation of a new contemporary identity. On the bright side this is often referred to as post-modern or New Age consciousness. But it has a darker side too whose aspects its apologists tend to disown or dismiss as vestiges of a former era. Insofar as I see these as integral to the post-modern identity as it is currently constituted, I will here, without prejudice to any future reconstitution that it might undergo, locate them where I feel they belong.

Perhaps the most important feature of this dark side is individualism. At the present time individual freedom reigns supreme and to propose anything which might depose the sovereign individual is looked on as an authoritarian heresy. There are important reasons why this has come about, and these should not be dismissed. We live in an age which has been bedevilled by different forms of totalitarianism in which individuals have, en masse, surrendered personal conscience to powers outside themselves. People have either committed or acquiesced to terrible crimes in the names of political parties and movements, and in the light of this we now look back at former times with especial vigilance for the seeds of such acquiescence in our forebears' allegiances to Church, Monarch, and Country. People have come to jealously guard the sovereignty of the individual conscience against all forms of authority which make claims on the secular

Individualism

world. Post-modernism has lain bare the political and psychological mechanisms whereby positions of secular power are constructed, so that any mystique which may have seduced the personal conscience into passive surrender has been dissolved. There is much good in this, but along with it has come a tendency to distrust *all* authority and to reduce it to a mere expression of the consensual collective conscience at any particular time, a reduction which equates authority with merely contingent power. With the removal of the executors of *traditional* authority, the symbols of *absolute* authority have also been dissolved, and the world itself has come to be seen as no more than the outcome of physical laws and the actions of the multitude of subjective wills which inhabit it. Although post-modernism has tended to reject modernism's materialist viewpoint in favour of a more spiritual one, so far it has, by and large, continued to see the world as an organic outgrowth of spontaneity and subjective creativity. How the individual adapts his desires to his physical and psychological environment is seen to be limited only by his own imagination and by legal prohibitions designed to secure the safety of all. Meanwhile, the prescribing of behavioural norms consistent with a perceived universal human nature has come to be seen as beyond the proper provenance of secular authority, and that has led to an almost universal individualism, guided only by personal desire and the mutual conditioning of interpersonal relationships.

One problem arising from this individualism is that its great emphasis on subjective measures of satisfaction at the expense of faith in tradition and trust of others, has meant that the wisdom normally held by elders in more traditional societies, which can save the young from repeating age-old mistakes, has been stripped of authority in the modern West. Sexual relationship based on trial and error has made it very difficult for people to make the lifelong commitment necessary for successful marriage. Divorce rates here are very high and couples are as likely to cohabit informally as to enter into marriage. Whilst we undoubtedly continue to value personal loyalty, the way we now think of this makes individualistic assumptions. If a couple's respective careers are pulling them in different directions it may be deemed selfish for either to expect affection or attachment to hold the other back. In place of the traditional marriage bond has arisen the modern transactional relationship. It lasts as long as it functions well, but as soon as things start to go seriously wrong then a split is on the cards. To suffer one's partner's failings is to be given a poor deal. One's relationship has become a bad transaction which could be legitimately terminated at any time.

Sexuality is no longer seen to properly belong in the marital home but has become an ever more widely accepted source of entertainment with a booming pornography industry netting millions of dollars every year. The post-modern individual is, to an unprecedented degree, sexually self-contained. Thanks to chemical contraception and more recently with the "day after" pill, chemical abortion, sex in today's world can be enjoyed without consequences and without love. In such a climate the emotional bonds of sexual love are easily trivialised and seen as no more than transitional pains along the

Transactional sex

bumpy road of sexual gratification. And if a modern young woman has the misfortune to become pregnant against her wishes, then the abortionist is at hand to relieve her of her problem.

The therapeutic treatment of morality

For the fortunate amongst us this way of life is well regulated and it is expected that things will run quite smoothly. If they don't then it is probably our own fault and therapy will be the appropriate answer. Here our hang-ups will be identified and our symptoms diagnosed before we are taught how better to manage our feelings in conformity with the respect and decorum deemed appropriate by our therapist's particular "take" on things. And what more can we expect from our therapist when the morals and mores of our cultural milieu are governed entirely by each person's "take" on things?

Criminal despair

For the less well adjusted things go smoothly less often. Restrained only by the proximity of others pursuing their own self-interests there are many amongst us who are frequently inclined to change the rules. If the game is individual satisfaction, by whose authority are the rules of the game to be played? That of those who are already doing very well out of it? But surely it is obvious that they want things to carry on just as they are. They are the principal beneficiaries. They have a vested interest. What if I have no faith in them? So goes what must be a common train of thought in the minds of many who are less fitted to play the present post-modernity game. And what do they do next? They cheat. They steal. They swindle. They defraud. They take. And sometimes, in despair, they kill themselves because they cannot bear to live in our society any longer.

My picture is incomplete but it is sufficient to create the impression I want to give. I do not believe it to be exaggerated except that in condensing numerous familiar aspects of contemporary life into a narrow field of focus it necessarily intensifies the image.

Now what has Buddhism to do with all of this? After all most Buddhists follow a rather strict moral discipline and aim to avoid harming any other sentient being. They are keenly aware of the interrelatedness of living beings and recognise the profound reach and range of immoral acts. Why do I point an accusing finger at Buddhism? I do so because I believe the love and compassion exemplified by Buddhists is an expression of their created humanity, not of their doctrine, whereas the Buddhist doctrine's underlying understanding of human nature is an erroneous expression of human intellect involving a self-manipulative spiritual reductionism which I believe is attractive to the post-modern identity. Buddhism in fact has often adapted its moral and ethical disciplines to different Asiatic societies, and is once again adapting itself, this time to the moral conventions of the post-modern West. In that process we have already seen numerous instances of highly respected teachers acting inappropriately in sexual matters. One famous tantric master, as well as being well known for his alcoholism was also widely referred to as a spiritual stud, so liberal was his sexuality.

The Buddhist justification of self-manipulation

Buddhism's moral relativism

53

Morality as convention

But this should not surprise us for in Buddhism the true nature of all things is seen either as the unconditioned or as the inconceivable Absolute. Morality and ethical behaviour are seen in terms of conventionality, and convention varies from society to society. What is noteworthy in the previous example is that the teacher's behaviour was deemed acceptable by his students who rationalised that he was behaving in that way in order to break their attachment to dualistic thinking, a view which certainly fits with Buddhism's understanding of conditioned existence and of its own most deeply held goal - liberation from suffering. Even where Buddhism recognises mandala principle, the spontaneous formation of coherent entities by the Absolute, there remains the sense in which the concrete is a mere manifestation of a more fundamentally real essence whose nature, being lawful rather than free, *creates* nothing but *manifests* everything[8].

Mandala principle

It is easy to highlight Buddhism's moral weakness by comparing it with Catholic views on sexuality. Where the Catholic believes that we have an irreducible God-given human nature, Buddhism believes we have only a karmically formed human nature. Where, morally speaking, the Catholic believes self-perfection to lie in obedience to the nature God intended for us, the Buddhist believes that it lies in non-attachment, which is to dwell in the unconditioned even while our present embodiment runs its karmically determined course. And while it cannot be denied that between the Catholic and the Buddhist there is a degree of overlap in the practise of non-attachment, it

54

also cannot be denied that the two are pervaded by a wholly different spirit and intention.

The Catholic recognises that sexual difference *defines* our humanity, and does not seek to marginalise it. The post-modern Buddhist on the other hand, often seeks to employ Buddhism's teaching of non-self in the service of feminist egalitarianism. Gender is seen as accidental to the human being's unconditioned essence. And since even biological gender is regarded as incidental to one's true nature so much less is one's social conditioning regarded as essential. Sexual identity thus becomes a matter of personal preference not necessarily connected to one's biological form. With this understanding, wrought in the heat of her struggle against men's exploitation, the radical feminist has sought to create herself anew in images of her own choosing. In this venture whereby the individual woman becomes the measure of her own worth every lifestyle becomes an expression of woman's nature, from priest to porn star, from business executive to caring mother. The only real taboo is that she does not intrude uninvited into someone else's life, the assumption being that as sovereign individuals we exist independently. The begrudged exceptions are the state and children, the state because it is only through it that individuals can become immediately independent of each other, and children because they cannot but be dependently intrusive on their parents and who simply by being themselves demonstrate the wholly artificial nature of the post-modern woman's "right to choose". One may be able to use contraception to *avoid* the consequences of having sex. And one may be able to resort to abortion to *undo* the consequences of

Catholic celebration of sexual compliment-arity

The myth of the right to choose

having sex. But without these fabrications parenthood follows sex as naturally as night follows day, and one's "right to choose" is unceremoniously swept away lest it degenerate into the right to ignore one's children's needs. Against the primacy of interdependence the post-modern emphasis on peoples' right to choose when and when not to accept the natural consequences of sexuality, is seen by the Catholic as a collectively held self-deception.

New Age man In our age of sexual egalitarianism, what goes for the goose goes for the gander, whether that is good for them both or not. Typically, post-modern man is "created" in the image of his female counterpart, but interestingly he doesn't seem to fare as well on it. For whereas a girl, no matter what she believes, will sooner or later come to bear the maternal burdens of womanhood, even if that only be the menstrual cycle, a boy will not naturally become a man. He will certainly grow in physical stature and come to experience sexual desire, or become a soldier and kill for his country, but these will not make him a man. For it is the call to fatherhood that turns boy into man, even though he may never have a wife or sire a child. While the natural imposition of motherhood upon a woman is over-whelming, there exists no such natural imposition of *Fatherhood* fatherhood upon men. Rather, fatherhood is called into being by words spoken to a man by his loved ones, and in the form of a demand placed upon him as a boy by his *The elders'* elders because they love him and wish to welcome him *welcome* into the brotherhood of fatherly men, who are warriors as well as farmers, celibates as well as lovers. Without that imposition, a boy is on his own unsupported, prey to his every impulse, insecure and nowhere to go. Without that

56

hurdle which by being leapt transports the boy into *The necessary leap* manhood, what chance does he have, on his own, of becoming a man?

What does a boy gain from the right to choose at a time *Denying the boy* when what he needs most is to be *denied* the right to choose! When it is time, without that denial he will forever remain a boy! It is not enough for him to be given the same set of rules as a girl. This is to deny both his strengths and his weaknesses. It is not enough to give him the same ground rules as she, to do what he wants as long as he is not dishonest, not hurtful to others, and so on. For what that involves for him is not the same as it involves for a girl. The girl is fated by nature to become a woman. She cannot naturally avoid the procreative deluge to come. The boy, in contrast, can never cultivate his manhood if we believe that one day it will come naturally to him. For the boy it must be hurdles all the way, together with overflowing love. Only these together allow him to feel *Love trials* secure and truly loved. It has nothing to do with competitive machismo. The boy undergoing his society's puberty rite is not in a competition with his peers. He is submitting his will to the authority that wisdom and love *Submission to authority* confer upon his elders. And all that is required is that he *does* submit. He need do no more than enough. Compare this with the pervasive sense of inadequacy in our modern societies in which young men seem *never* to feel that they have done enough to prove their manhood, a sentiment we see over and again leading to outbursts of hatred and violence, the so-called yob culture our politicians complain about. But our young men are responding honestly to the situation they are in. Their elders, in bending over backwards to accept them for what they *are*, neglect to demand that they become what they *should be*. And so what is left for them but to try desperately to initiate themselves, using their imaginations to set their own trials and tests of endurance. Our outrage at the haphazard and savage results of these ritual heroic quests is disingenuous. We are harsh judges who would rather see brave but leaderless young men defamed and deformed by our judgements than ourselves dare to become the leaders that *we* should be.

The chaos of self-initiation

Masculation of women

In emphasising this distinction between boys and girls I do not wish to make light of the difficulties girls face in growing up, merely to stress that the weight of nature is on the side of girl's maturing into responsible women. This is testified to by popular culture's apparent double standard in the different degrees of reprehension it reserves for negligent mothers and fathers. Whereas a father's flight from responsibility is regarded as merely deplorable, a mother's is often regarded as an evil betrayal of her own nature, which is deemed far less excusable. However, as men's natural remoteness from childbirth is matched by women's growing artificial remoteness from it through ever-proliferating technological and political innovations, girls more and more face similar difficulties to boys in submitting to the natural meaning of their sexuality.

Rite of passage to sexual order

Ironically every primitive society shows through its puberty rites, that it knows what ours has so evidently forgotten – that the differing traditional social identities of men and women are not merely products of social conditioning but conform aesthetically to the inherently sexual nature of mankind. The fullness of these differences is however hidden from the new-born who can only discover it during a childhood embraced and nurtured in the cradle of a society whose rational beauty, as opposed to its enslavement by the instincts, is a condition of mature human being. This is as true for our society as any primitive one and it is because of this that we have the power to truly behave *unnaturally*. To avoid such a corruption, the way we shape our children's lives must merely *seal* their proper natures. But that would require *Socialisation as* our perfection as elders and can be no more than a goal we *a seal of the* set for ourselves. The puberty rite can be seen to not only *natural* place a demand upon the uninitiated, but upon the elders too who must strive to make their society one worth entering into. At the very least it must be an initiation into the obligation to honour the fullness of one's true sexual nature, which is one's family and the community to which it belongs. Until recent times Buddhism has been able to avoid explicating these problems because wherever it took root there existed a strong society with already ancient customs and traditions which Buddhists respected. In the moral chaos of the contemporary world, with no established tradition to lean on, things are not so easy. What we are seeing is the incorporation of Buddhism into the anti-dogmatic dogma of post-modernity. It lends itself to this very well.

Homosexuality, for instance, for the post-modern Buddhist *The offence of* is a non-issue since it no longer offends convention, and *homosexuality* has no necessary deleterious effects on either one's karma or on one's true essence. For the Catholic, on the other hand, it is a very serious moral offence since it contradicts and corrupts the inherently heterosexual nature of sexuality[9].

The post-modern may object at this point that I have conceded that the sexual persona, being called into being, especially in men, by the power of the word, is contingent and not essential to one's true nature. But this objection seems valid to him only because he thinks of the word as a purely human thing, a morally arbitrary product of natural evolution. For the Catholic the human word is only isolated if man himself chooses to make it so by cutting himself off from God. The bible teaches that God created the world by the power of His Word and that the moral task confronting humanity consists in being obedient to this Word. In less theological language, for much of the time this simply means doing what you know in your heart to be right. The word which calls forth man- or womanhood from the child transcends the arbitrariness of social conditioning by its universal propriety. Though it is spoken by the guardian elders, it is inspired by the profundity of the Divine. Unfortunately the heart is easily overcome by the calculating mind, and the desire for beauty overwhelmed by selfish lust.

Both the Buddhist and the Catholic know that if nature is left to take its course a foetus will develop into a complete human person. However where the Catholic sees this development as the intention of God's creative will, a way of looking at reality which lets him see things in their wholeness, the Buddhist sees it as the operation of the law of karma which in itself has no *moral* authority. Morality is its product not its nature. It is just cause and effect. That a fertilised human egg is destined to become a complete human being is a fact known to both Buddhist and Catholic alike, but for the Buddhist this is merely a contingent fact whereas for the Catholic it is a proper one. For the Catholic it isn't just *probable* that, natural law being what it is, the fertilised egg will grow to become an actualised human person. For him, in whom the aesthetic sense is at least equal in strength to the analytic, the fertilised egg already is that person. The analytic mind alone, which explains the development from embryo to adult in terms of sequential causality, tends to fixate on the present actuality in a manner which excludes the whole lifespan. The lifespan comes to be seen as no more than the probable result of a present and actual cause. But saying that the lifespan is likely to take place is not the same as saying that it *should* take place. And without that sense of what should be, why should we ourselves not intervene to change the course of events? Physical or karmic law is neither proper nor improper. It is merely matter of fact. And it is that matter of factness which gives Buddhist morality a degree of ambiguity. The Buddhist avoids harming sentient beings, no matter how small and insignificant they may be, because he wishes to avoid suffering, both in himself and in others. But this has nothing to do with his or their *rightful* existence, and that weakens his position with regard to the rights of the embryo. For if he can be convinced by modern science that the embryo is incapable of suffering due to its physical immaturity then what remaining objection can he have to abortion?

Narrowness of the analytic mind

Rightful existence

The Catholic, in contrast, sees the question of abortion very simply. The ultimate author of natural propriety is God the Creator. The natural intention of human conception is the living of a human life from beginning to end, and the measure of the human being's worth is the innate goodness of his whole existence, not the momentary effectiveness of his present functions. As a consequence of this view the Catholic recognises abortion as a form of murder and regards it as morally repellent.

Abortion as murder

Buddhism's non-theism causes moral error

The Buddhist does not share the Catholic's sense of natural propriety because he does not believe it to possess any greater authority than that of the law of karma. The propriety of nature is no more for him than the propriety of *past* karma, and though he cannot change the results of that he can, he believes, avoid repeating the same actions in the future. For the Christian something is missing here - the wholehearted affirmation of life for its own sake as the glorification of God's creativity. This basic lack of genuine love for creatureliness, implicit at least in the Buddhist doctrine, leaves the mind which is steeped in the values of Judaism, Christianity or Islam unsatisfied. Indeed I would suggest that the emergence of the Buddha Nature schools with their understanding of ordinary reality as the display of the Absolute, shows this dissatisfaction to have been present and active within the Buddhist tradition itself. I believe that Buddhism's relativism and its belief in rebirth can undermine peoples' appreciation of each other's uniqueness, and it is remarkable though not surprising how easily Buddhism has adapted to the individualism of the post-modern West. Where modernist individualism trod the individual's unique value underfoot

The incompleteness of Buddhist compassion

Loss of uniqueness

in the quest for universal independence, post-modernism is treading it underfoot under the pretext of *inter*dependence, which the Buddhist doctrine explicates very comprehensively. Typically, the post-modern takes up the Buddhist emphasis on interdependence without Buddhism's traditional moral strictures on sexual misconduct. The ideal post-modern individual doesn't get hung up about grief when a relationship ends, but rather, feels the pain of it, lets the healing process do its thing, and moves on in the hubris of life. The bonds of love are seen essentially as evolved functions which can and should be managed by the individual in his particular quest for personal growth and fulfilment. More and more, life becomes a matter of surfing the waves of incessant change, and those who perfect the art without getting stuck in the mud are the cool ones who people envy and admire. Admittedly, this is a caricature to make the point, and all but the cool ones themselves will laugh at it and recognise its absurdity. But the reality is worse because though being more subtle, more concealed, more inclined to self-parody, its values are nonetheless those of the caricature.

To the Catholic this is a nightmare. When, as a child, you need your mother's and father's love, there cannot be and never will be any possible substitute for that love. It is true that in relation to your material needs you could be fostered or be adopted by new parents. But the love of your new parents would never be a substitute for the love of your mother and father. For love is not a mere need which could be satisfied by anyone. Love is always for a unique person whom to lose is to lose forever. It is a marvellous terrible thing. And it is because the Catholic

The uniqueness of the individual

Inseparability of the marriage bond

Church understands this that it insists that the bond of marriage, once validly established, becomes inseparable. This is not an example of stubborn conservatism on the Church's part. It is said because the Church knows what true conjugal love is. The beginning of its unbounded generosity, given by two unique persons to each other, seals them into a single intertwined identity making them unfit to be with anyone else. Their mutual belonging can only end when one of them is no longer alive to receive the other's love. The real irreversibility of that bond cannot properly be understood by one who sees his manifest nature as accidental to his essence, which view arises out of the notion of conditioned existence being the result of ignorant self-clinging. For to the extent that he identifies with his essence, then to that extent does he dissociate with his own manifest uniqueness and with it the capacity for the fullness of conjugal love. Those Buddhist traditions of later periods which deny that our manifest nature is necessarily accidental to our Absolute Essence, may have a more humane view than the above, but have achieved it, I believe, only by a radical re-vision of the Buddha's original understanding.

Christianity for Buddhists

Why should someone drawn to Buddhism even give a moment's thought to Christianity? Well, initially, as I hope to have shown, because Christian thought is able to mount a convincing critique of Buddhist doctrine on the ground that by practising a form of spiritual reductionism it is lacking in humane values. But why would the reader give any credence to that charge unless those values were present within himself and capable of judging it in their own light?

This is just what I have come to believe. I think now that the aesthetic sense, by which I mean the faculty of appreciating beauty or perfection, is of the utmost importance in human life. I believe it both precedes and enables reason. It gives reason something to do. Without aesthetic value reason would be a mere instrument of instinct, something which perhaps increased one's efficiency without deepening one's sense of propriety. The aesthetic sense orientates you to what is proper, to what ought to be, to what is normal and rightly ordered. It not only allows you to participate in the ordering of the world, it positively urges you to do so, for it is not simply a passive faculty but an affective one. Inasmuch as one assents to anything on the grounds of its perfection, one is accepting the validity of aesthetic value as a necessary determinant of one's understanding and knowledge of the world.

The aesthetic sense

The religious value of beauty I think that a scientist's striving to arrive at a satisfactory theory involves the aesthetic sense as one of its deepest motives, but its emotional ambience differs to that of religious devotion. Science is a deepening of our understanding of the physical workings of the world, either simply to satisfy the desire to understand, or to further human empowerment in pursuit of its interests. Religious understanding seeks to facilitate religious devotion as the proper relationship of man to the source and origin of his existence. The human being as scientist strives to be objective, and in confirming the validity of his theories deliberately excludes the aesthetic sense from his empirical observations. The human being as religious subject allows aesthetic value to pervade all aspects of his consciousness and knows life in terms of it.

The unity of science and religion So why does the aesthetic sense sometimes lead towards science and at other times towards religious devotion? I think it is because aesthetic value is a unity of different aspects which can, if the individual so chooses, be cultivated separately. However, not only is there no necessary antithesis between science and religion, but each is impoverished without the other. When science breaks free of aesthetic restraint its methods of analysis and dissection turn into acts of violence against nature. When religion ignores science it founds itself upon worldly ignorance and must soon resort to irrationality to defend its increasingly indefensible claims.

The moral is the proper The religious idiom seeks to satisfy our wish to relate properly with metaphysical realities. In doing so it expresses a profound sense of mystery as it contemplates

66

the origin, nature and authority of things. That things *are* so is an obvious empirical fact. But that things *should* be so is a moral as well as a scientific question and should not be delegated to the scientist to answer. The moral aspect to the question is the more profound since the way we each conform to and order our world is the answer we give to the most fundamental questions we each are confronted with: who am I? what am I? how should I live my life? Our answer determines who and what we are and involves our most intimate knowledge and understanding of what the world is and how it ought to be.

From this perspective a thing is no mere thing. A thing is a *The proper has* way. And insofar as it involves the world in its own being *moral authority* it is a way of *ordering* the world, hence my reference to the *authority* of things. Things have authority over me to the extent that I consent to their ordering my being and the life that I live. If a thing is perceived as a mere empirical fact one unwittingly fails to notice that it is capable of exercising authority in the world. To see no more than power in a thing's existence is to pre-empt the moral question that its existence poses. Mere power is morally arbitrary whereas authority is a rightful exercise of power over others. A thing's existence is affirmed by others *Natural* when they recognise its rightful exercise of power. In this *authority as* affirmation others accept it as proper that its existence *elicitation of* affects them and contributes to their own particular nature, *natural potential* even where the thing is a source of food or sustenance to be consumed and thus brought to an end. It may seem strange to think of the killing of a prey animal by a predator as an affirmation of the prey's existence, but in an important sense that is precisely what it is. All things being equal the predator might have been a herbivore, but things are not equal. The predator is indeed a predator and discovers the full meaning of its given nature in its response to its prey. The prey elicits that response just as surely as the predator initiates it. Thus, genetic pre-adaptation notwithstanding, the prey animal is the final author of the predator's predatory nature, while in turn the predator is the one who finally brings out the true nature of the prey. Each has its proper place in the predator-prey relationship and discovers its particular meaning only in that relationship. Having said that, I can think of no reason to suppose that in the case of animals there is any great awareness of the propriety of nature. The animal is so woven into the fabric of nature that it has little need of such awareness. It is completely overwhelmed by natural propriety. Awareness of propriety, which belongs to the aesthetic faculty, is above all a human thing which seems necessary due to the weight of free will in human nature. It is only because of free will, situated in the midst of natural order, that human life encounters moral problems and requires awareness of propriety. If one is advised, for instance, that a particular area is teeming with dangerous wild animals and one ignores that advice, taking one's family there for a picnic, one's inappropriate behaviour amounts to criminal negligence, an act of immorality.

Moral authority as human recognition of natural authority

So far, the only authority I have considered is the authority of natural things over each other. This authority has operated as a rule of nature. When we come to consider mankind however things take on a different light. It is simply a fact that the authority of natural things places man at the pinnacle of nature's hierarchy. Nature ultimately presents human beings with the moral problems of monarchical rule since, as the first book of the bible relates, man truly has dominion over this world. Human nature's very strength is its ability to step outside of every ecological niche in order to overcome all forms of natural limitation, only to discover that in the end it is limited by everything taken as a whole. In order to maintain the health of the whole the human being must act monarchically, never identifying with any single one of nature's parts. Thus the question of what the individual creature is and what it can rightfully expect of life is connected to the question of what nature is and how man should rule it. This finally raises the question of ultimate authority. Is man's authority derived solely from his position within the natural world, arisen quite accidentally according to the random mutations of the evolutionary process? Or does the order of the natural world derive from a higher authority still, one to which man, for all his ingenuity and adaptability, must always be subordinate?

Moral problem of monarchical rule

Ultimate authority

An evolutionary perspective would say that just as the form of any particular species is a conservative a priori biological convention, so is the aesthetic faculty a conservative a priori psychological convention. The aesthetic faculty will be seen as merely a part of our psychophysiological makeup, evolved over thousands of years. The secular person who accepts it does so at face value as an act of faith or basic self-confidence. His senses of right and wrong, beauty and ugliness, perfection and fault, are all part of what he discovers himself to be. They are in him and they are him. His sense of rightness tells him that his sense of rightness is right. In him the moral

Beauty as convention

The individual as his own authority

and aesthetic faculties are their own authority and require no higher authority to justify them.

The arbitrariness of individual authority

The problem with this view is that his rational mind could just as easily conclude that his sense of rightness is a sentimental luxury indulged for old time's sake, or that he personally is an exception to the rule and is a natural born killer or whatever. He cannot escape the sense that morality, along with everything else in the universe, is ultimately meaningless. Without any moral value life is reduced to a compulsive but essentially absurd struggle. Whatever he feels about existence is no more than his subjective feeling, his personal preference. Existence in itself is quite empty of the values he places upon it. The only right is what the individual believes to be right, and so morality quickly becomes no more than an exercise in power. Inevitably, in this environment, the aesthetic faculty eventually withers to be replaced by a conflict-driven consciousness in which personal uniqueness becomes little more than market packaging of a shared herd identity.

Beauty as illusion

On reflection it can be seen that the notion of self-authorising moral value is logically incoherent. For if the right and the beautiful do not exist outside of ourselves then our knowledge of right and beauty is only a self-indulgent solipsistic illusion to be transcended by wisdom. The greatest achievement of wisdom would be a state of ultimate amorality - which is just what we see in Zen, Vajrayana Buddhism and other mystical paths. But who, apart from the spiritual aspirants themselves, really believes this? No honest person will admit to it. The Zen master who teaches ultimate amorality by being cruel to a cat, to most people is just a deluded fool being cruel to a cat! His misplaced amorality is just plain simple immorality.

We believe we *know* something of the world when we encounter rightness and beauty. We act upon that belief in the ways we relate to others. What we assume in practise we should admit in principle, and if we concede that much at least then we must allow ourselves a less subjective and more realistic train of thought. Unless a thing is intended it is no more than an accident. For a thing to be deemed perfect it must conform to a nature which is proper to it. And this proper nature must be conferred upon it by something prior to itself. Now we might suppose that this prior something was the world of the past which spawned this new thing. But unless that world also was conforming to some prior intention then the argument would simply have landed at the feet of another thing whose own perfection had yet to be demonstrated. If we are to avoid an infinite regress we must follow the chain of intentions back to some original wilful source, which takes us beyond the natural world to the supernatural. Why must it be wilful and why must it be supernatural? It must be wilful because being the origin of all that exists nothing can precede it, and its actions therefore cannot be subject to any cause. And it is just this freedom from causality that makes it supernatural.

The reality of beauty

The wilfulness of the supernatural

The foregoing argument is not an *absolute* proof of God's existence, but it is a demonstration of how our acceptance of God's existence satisfies our deepest longings for love

Our need for God

and beauty, so much so that if we deny the existence of God we deny the value of love and beauty. In becoming mere personal preferences they lose their meaning. It is then that we begin to realise once again that the problem of Divinity cannot be reduced to an affair of the intellect since what we are deciding is the life or death of those qualitative values which give our life its deepest meaning.

Our certainty of God

Love and beauty would be meaningless without God's will, but since we know on our own authority that they are not meaningless we can know with equal authority that God's will exists and seeks the natural perfection of this world of ours .

The goodness of creation

And so we arrive at the "first noble truth" of the bible. It is not, as in Buddhism, the truth of suffering. It is the truth that in the beginning God created the heavens and the earth, the land and the sea, the moon, the sun and the stars, the plants, the animals and man. And looking upon His creation He saw that it was good. This is the starting point for the Jew, the Christian and the Muslim. Man's downfall is not his creation, the beginning of his self-clinging, as it is understood in the Buddhist tradition. On the contrary, his existence is a good to be enjoyed.

In the image of God

Man – the king of paradise

The second noble truth of the bible is that man was created in the image of God and was destined to live in paradise having dominion over all God's creatures. Here is proclaimed the uniqueness of man, the Godlike universality of his mind embodied in animal flesh, which in its lordly command of nature, its original intimate knowledge of God, and its openness to His grace, allowed him to enjoy life as unending paradise. Here is proclaimed

72

the monarchical principle, whereby man used the understanding of his intellect to nurture and harmonise, in accordance with God's will, the world he had been given to live in. If God it was who planted the garden and created its occupants from the clay of the earth, it was man's lot to be its gardener and caring husband.

The third noble truth is that it is not good for man to live alone and for that reason woman was created out of his own flesh. *The two will be as one flesh* When man and woman leave their mother and father to become husband and wife the two become as one flesh, and to separate them thereafter is an evil and violent act. This remains so even if the one who separates them is one of the partners themselves. Those who believe Christianity to be irredeemably corrupted with guilt about sex would do well to remember that in Genesis man's sexuality is given to him, male and female, as a source of pleasure and companionship, before his fall from grace. The Christian feels guilt not over his sexuality but over his failure to fulfil its promise. To the Christian, man is wholly sexual. One is *defined* as a human being by one's gender. A human being is either a man or a woman, not an androgenous soul or stream of existence temporarily inhabiting a male or female body. For the Christian, man and woman belong together, the fullness of their love accepting each other wholly for as long as they live. Such is man's created nature, and with the exception of exclusive devotion to God, it is in obedience to this that he perfects himself.

The fourth noble truth is man's freedom which gave him the power to act wrongly and that by so doing he was cast *The fall* out of paradise. The bible story tells us that having created both Adam and Eve and placed them in the paradisical garden of Eden, God commanded that they may eat of all the trees there except one - the tree of knowledge of good and evil, "For if you do, on that day you will surely die." Alas, one day, Eve, tempted by the serpent, picked the fruit of the forbidden tree and, having eaten it gave some to Adam who followed her example. On learning of this God demanded an explanation. Adam blamed it all on Eve while she blamed it upon the serpent. Seeing that they may now move on to the tree of life and live on, in sin, for ever, God now expelled them from paradise. Eve, he said, would suffer an increase in the pains of childbirth and be subject to her husband's domination. Adam, he said, would from then on have to work by the sweat of his brow to make the land yield up his wants. His life would be one of hard toil until he died and returned to the earth from which he was made. The serpent would become the enemy of man, man forever in fear of it striking at his heel and it afraid of him who in hatred would crush it. God then placed a terrible sword-wielding angel at the gates of paradise to prevent man from entering again.

The reductionist challenge to Divine Authority

What are we to make of this story, so rich in symbol and meaning? We must start with the fruit of the tree of knowledge of good and evil. Why was this forbidden to man? It was forbidden because of what it offered, the very thing which made it so tempting. It promised to make man like God in knowing good and evil, and it is significant that the serpent understood this very well. For what was at issue here was Divine Authority. On the one side was God the creator, the very source of all that existed and was good, by virtue of which only He could know and proclaim good and evil. On the other side was the serpent, a transparent metaphor for the Uroboros, that most subtle of God's creations, tempting man to arrogate divine knowledge unto himself. The Uroboros, then, as it is employed in the biblical book of Genesis, is both a symbol of the subtle interdependence of God's creations, and at the same time is a symbol of the satanically inspired spiritual reductionism which pervaded those cultures surrounding Judaism, especially the Babylonian which captured the Jewish people and in which the Yahwistic writer of Genesis is thought to have lived. What the story is telling us is that by turning his back on Divine Authority in pursuit of his own lust for power, man became unfit to exercise his dominion over the world, and unfit to receive God's grace. In putting himself before Divine harmony paradise was lost and man's worldly existence became a lonely fearful march towards death.

"Hide not Thy face for oppression is hard upon me."

The fifth and last noble truth is that man can be saved from his fallen state by following in the Way of Christ, a Way which, as the Word of God, has always been there but which became incarnate in the person of Jesus of Nazareth. Jesus' simple but profound message, to love the Lord our God with all our heart and with all our mind, and to love our neighbour as ourself, is God's answer to man's suffering. Jesus - the Way, the Truth and the Life - lived faithfully according to his own teaching, despite his rejection by the world and his deliverance to the cross

Our Saviour: arisen from the death of fallenness to eternal life

75

upon which he was crucified. Instead of that lust for power, that reductionistic ambition, which has led us to our present predicament and which we repeat every day in innumerable ways, Jesus showed us in the prayer He gave to us, what our proper relationship to God and his creation should be like:

"Our Father, who art in heaven, hallowed be thy name. Thy kingdom come. Thy will be done, on earth as it is in heaven. Give us this day our daily bread, and forgive us our trespasses as we forgive those who trespass against us. Lead us not into temptation, but deliver us from evil. Amen."

Losing ourselves to Christ Here is the only way of relating to existence that befits the worldly kingship which is ours. Only man's loving surrender to the truths of creation and creatureliness can safeguard nature and himself from his own ubiquitous power. The gateway to heaven lies in establishing God's Kingdom here on earth, and this will be done not by trying to save ourselves but by losing ourselves to Christ, our Lord. Must we, in following Him, tread the path of karma-ending karma? No. We follow him by taking up our own particular cross and walking to the end of the road with Him in the certain hope that thereby we will be resurrected to eternal life.

Notes

1. "A Survey of Fundamentals" - first discourse of the Middle Collection, publ. Janus, 1992.
(Page 21)

2. The Buddha's understanding of self-emptiness was more profound than some of his later followers could comprehend. Some, such as the Sautrantikas and Sarvastivadins, thought there had to be some sort of worldly foundation to reality which was not susceptible to the Buddha's analysis. This conviction led the Sautrantikas to postulate the twin notions of atomism and momentariness, and the Sarvastivadins the idea that things, for as long as they existed, possessed an unchanging substance. Atoms, or "partless particles" as the Sautrantikas called them, were supposed to be the most elementary building blocks of conditioned existence, whereas indivisible moments were said to be the basic units of time. But it was difficult to make these concepts work. A partless particle would be unchangeable and could not be affected by other particles. How, then, could such particles combine to form larger objects? Similarly, an indivisible moment could, in itself, contain no time. How, then, could a series of moments with no duration add up to a period of time? And with regard to the Sarvastivadin position, if things possessed an unchanging substance, how could they change? If one state of a thing leads causally to another, how can its substance be said to be unchanged? These kinds of arguments, which, incidentally, present as cogent a challenge to the Greek philosophers of atomism and substance as they did to their Buddhist counterparts, were put most forcefully by the Mahayanist philosopher, Nagarjuna, who, in posing them, re-asserted the profundity of the Buddha's teaching.
(Page 25)

3. These schools are generally rooted in the Yogachara tradition see "The Wisdom of the Buddha: The Samdhinirmocana Sutra", Dharma 1994.
(Page 27)

4. Yogachara thought - or Chittamatra - is usually refuted by proponents of the Madhyamika tradition, especially those of the Prasangika schools. See "Meditation on Emptiness", Jeffrey Hopkins, Wisdom 1996. Also see "Bodhicittavivarana" in "Master of Wisdom: Writings of the Buddhist Master Nagarjuna", Dharma 1986. (Page 29)

5. It is my belief that the Buddha held an implicit understanding of the unconditioned as Absoluteness, but steadfastly avoided any positive expression of that understanding since none is possible which would not lead his followers away from a full appreciation of its mystery. Many, such as David Kalupahana of the University of Hawaii, would dispute that belief and consider it to be an absolutist distortion of the Buddha's teaching (see appendix and bibliography). (Page 32)

6. See note 3. (Page 39)

7. "According to [Chittamatra] this manifold world is. . . mere consciousness . . . [They] claim that mind purified by a transformation in position [becomes] the object of its own specific [knowledge]. [But mind] that is past does not exist, [while] that which is future is nowhere discovered. [And] how can the present mind shift from place to place? . . . The alayavijnana does not appear the way it is. As it appears – it is not like that. Consciousness essentially lacks substance; it has no other basis [than insubstantiality]."

These verses of Nagarjuna from the Bodhicittavivarana, ("The Master of Wisdom: Writings of The Buddhist Master Nagarjuna", Lindtner, Dharma 1986) refute the Chittamatrin and Shentong notions of mind as the true essence of reality. Shentongpas claim to be immune from Nagarjuna's refutation on the grounds that it refers only to the *stream of consciousness* – the *alayavijnana*, whereas *they* believe there to be a non-conceptual mind beyond the stream of consciousness – the *alaya*. But for such a mind to mean anything at all it must be substantially existent, even if, like Aristotle's primary matter, it is phenomenally indeterminate. The above quote specifically refutes the existence of any substantial basis to the mind as such and *must*, I think, be seen as a refutation of the Shentong notion of alaya as the ground of Being. That is not, however, to refute the notion of a ground of Being entirely, but rather to equate it, as Nagarjuna appears to elsewhere, with Sunyata or Emptiness, as distinct from non-dual mind. (p41)

8. Whereas earlier Buddhists believed that all sentient beings were the results of ignorant self-clinging, even the body of one who had become a Buddha, later, Buddhists of the Tibetan Kagyu and Nyingma schools, believed that mandala principle and spontaneity were inherent in Buddha Nature. The combination of these two principles enlarged the notion of enlightened living whilst avoiding the belief in a creator God. Buddha Nature playfully gave rise to the phenomena we experience as mundane reality by way of the two impersonal principles of spontaneity and mandala. Our will was understood to have originated in this way, but in ignorance had embarked on the path of ignorant self-clinging which led to the formation of all the various realms of conditioned existence. Now, ignorant self-clinging was no longer seen as the sole formative principle, and one who, through his perfection of non-attachment and his suffusion with compassion for others, could align himself with the Buddha Nature's principles of spontaneity and mandala principle, and seek further existence in the service of others. His wish (pranidhana) was a different kind of formative principle in that its freedom from self-clinging caused no suffering.

Others of the Mahayana tradition, to which the Kagyupas and Nyingmapas belong, have different ways of understanding this more positive approach, but they all share their adherence to the bodhisattva vow to attain enlightenment for the benefit of others, and accept the historical diminution in status of the arhat, formerly thought to be the highest state of attainment prior to liberation without remainder (the passing away at death never to be reborn), to a position below that of the bodhisattva.
(Page 55)

9. This is not to deny that many individuals may be predisposed through natural genetic variation to be attracted to members of their own sex. What is being challenged is the reduction of the normative

heterosexual aesthetic to a mere statistical average of people's sexual preferences. To do so is to obscure the true meaning of sexuality and to substitute an egocentric rationalism for intuitive aesthetic intelligence. Though one' mature sexual persona is clearly a social construct, this does not mean that it is *only* a social construct. There is an inevitable tension between the individual's personal preferences and the natural sexual aesthetic, a tension which may involve disorder and suffering. The Church calls for compassion towards homosexuals whilst insisting on the normative nature of heterosexuality, and the disordered or sinful nature of homosexual acts.

(Page 60)

Appendix A

In trying to cover the subject of Buddhism in a brief and readable manner, it becomes necessary to generalise. And in generalising one runs the risk of misrepresenting everyone and satisfying no one. An area where this is most keenly felt concerns the nature of the *unconditioned*. Within Buddhism itself there is much disputation concerning this very point. Some will see as controversial my opening statement that Buddhism "cuts through the apparent solidity of the world until ultimately it seems so transparent that we no longer see the multitude of things as separate but as different aspects of one inconceivable being." Though this, I believe, is in keeping with the Buddha's teaching I realise that some will associate it with a specifically Shentong (emptiness-of-other) point of view and that to others it will sound more like Brahmanism, or Advaita Vedanta perhaps. Some will feel that my attribution to Buddhism of a view of things as momentary states of an indeterminate ground of self-existent being, ignores the fact that for the Buddha the whole of reality was as empty of self as its parts are.

Anticipating these reservations I should like to at least show that the general view that I expressed was not limited to the Kagyu Shentong tradition. It is true that throughout the Pali Canon the Buddha takes great pains to avoid making any statement similar to my own under consideration here, and that Tibetan Gelugpa Prasangikas adhere to that avoidance scrupulously. I believe this avoidance to be largely an expression of the Buddha's emphasis on personal knowledge of truth as distinct from conviction by hearsay. Release from suffering, he believed, could only come about through genuine knowledge, and in that respect he regarded metaphysical speculation and religiosity as mere opinion which only prolonged attachment and suffering. The unconditioned, for him, was not an idea but an experienced reality. What is at issue is how the reality of the unconditioned may be experienced. The view that I have adopted in this book is that although the unconditioned is real it can only be experienced negatively, that is, as a presence revealed by what is not it rather than as something experienced as an immediate object of the ordinary faculties of knowledge. At the same time I do not hesitate to refer to it as an actual reality whose nature is non-dual. This, I believe, is understood by Buddhists of most traditions, not just the Kagyu Shentongpas. For example:

"Rather than saying you have to believe in the Uncreated or in Ultimate Truth or in God, the Buddha pointed to what is created, born, originated. He taught that we should look at these created conditions because that is what we can see directly and learn from. He taught that the act of being mindful and awake to the created takes us to the Uncreated, *because we experience the created arising out of the Uncreated and going back into the Uncreated.* [my italics].

This experience of the Uncreated, at most an ineffable experience, the Buddha called nibbana (nirvana), which means a calm or coolness. It can sound almost like annihilation - no soul, no self, no God. It can sound really dreary, but that's not what the Buddha meant. He was pointing to the fact that these very unsatisfactory conditions, which are ever-changing, are not self. He was not making a doctrinal statement that there is no self and that we have to believe in no self, but he was pointing to the way whereby one can see the truth. As you watch the conditions of the body and mind you realise that they come and go; they change. There is no substance to them that you can extract and say 'This is mine.'"

This quote from his book "The Mind and the Way" by Ajahn Sumedho of the Theravadin tradition in Thailand (Rider, 1996, used by permission of The Random House Group Ltd), clearly shows a view of the unconditioned as something real, not a mere absence of reality. In that respect it is substantially in agreement with my opening statement. To give another example, the following, from "What the Buddha Taught" by the Sri Lankan Theravadin, the Venerable Dr Walpola Rahula (The Gordon Fraser Gallery, 1959, permission granted by One World Publishing), takes up a similar position:

"Now you will ask: But what is Nirvana? . . . The only reasonable reply to give to the question is that it can never be answered completely and satisfactorily in words, because human language is too poor to express the real nature of the Absolute Truth or Ultimate Reality which is Nirvana . . . Nevertheless we cannot do without language. But if Nirvana is to be expressed and explained in positive terms, we are likely to immediately grasp an idea associated with those terms which may be quite the contrary. Therefore it is generally expressed in negative terms - a less dangerous mode perhaps. So it is often referred to by such terms as . . . extinction of thirst . . . uncompound . . . unconditioned . . . absence of desire . . . cessation . . . [or] blowing out.

. . . Because Nirvana is thus expressed in negative terms, there are many who have got a wrong notion that it is negative and expresses self-annihilation. Nirvana is definitely no annihilation of self, because there is no self to annihilate. If at all, it is annihilation of the illusion, of the false idea of self.

It is incorrect to say that Nirvana is negative or positive. The ideas of 'negative' and 'positive' are relative and are within the realm of duality. These terms cannot be applied to Nirvana, Absolute Truth, which is beyond duality and relativity.

. . . the Buddha unequivocally uses the word Truth in place of Nibbana . . . Now what is Absolute Truth? According to Buddhism, the Absolute Truth is that there is nothing absolute in the world, that everything is relative, conditioned and impermanent, and that there is no unchanging, everlasting, absolute substance like Self, Soul or Atman, within or without. This is the Absolute Truth . . . It is interesting and useful to rememeber the Mahayanist view of Nirvana as not being different from Samsara. The same thing is Samsara or Nirvana according to the way you look at it.

. . . Nirvana is not the result of anything . . . Truth is not a result nor an effect . . . TRUTH *IS*. NIRVANA *IS*."

Again, the unconditioned is depicted here as a reality, not an absence of reality. The real difficulty presented to anyone wishing to speak of the unconditioned lies, as Walpola Rahula makes clear, in its non-duality. It is quite easy to recognise the impossibility of capturing the nature of non-duality using human language since all language is inherently dualistic. It is axiomatic that any lingual reference to non-duality will be symbolic or metaphorical and will always be open to deconstruction in strictly logical terms. It is less easy to see that *all* experience is dualistic and suffers the same limitation with regard to non-duality. It should be noted, then, that the intellect is able to penetrate the nature not only of language but also that of the dualistic or determinate existence to which language refers. When the intellect is applied in this way, all conditioned existence, whether subjective or objective, is seen to be empty of inherent existence. What remains when this emptiness is perceived is obviously some sort of reality to which our experience, and more importantly, our will, belongs. The question is: what is the nature of that reality and in what way does our experience belong to it? It is here that things start to get particularly difficult.

The problem lies very simply in the fact that whilst, as the Gelugpa Prasangika shows, the appearance of reality is entirely illusory and refers to nothing inherently real at all, the appearances themselves, though illusory, are nevertheless real insofar as they are irrefutably experienced in the present. The Gelugpa Prasangika explains that, yes, present appearances *are* actual, but not because they exist inherently as the things they appear to be; rather, because they are the results of causes and conditions. Following the Buddha, his way of investigating reality is empirical and analytical, hence he avoids all metaphysical speculation and does not attribute things' existence to some substance of their own or of Absolute Being.

To use an illustration, if a red square in a computer programme is dropped onto a red background, it ceases to be a square at all. Without the relative difference in colour, the figure merges with the background so that both become one unified field of redness which is neither figure nor ground. Clearly the square depended for its squareness on the relationship between its redness and a background of non-redness. It did not depend on its own substantial existence. If one considers reality as a whole from the perspective of being per se, all things merge into one unified field of Being. This Being, unlike the field of redness which can still be perceived in relation to non-redness, encompasses everything and cannot be perceived in relation to anything at all. In itself, therefore, it cannot appear as an existent. It is wholly indeterminate and hidden in its own infinity.

This is amply clarified by Professor Herbert Guenther when, in his book "Wholeness Lost and Wholeness Regained" (SUNY, 1994), he makes an important distinction between wholeness and totality:

"Let us bear in mind that wholeness - the Being-that-is-not in Padmasambhava's words - is not the same as totality. The latter can be summed up by the parts that make up a totality as an objective closure; the former cannot. It is a single indivisible and irreducible reality whose 'oneness' or 'uniqueness' may be likened to a single quantum state that in its not being a thing (whether material or immaterial) is an 'openness' - a (dynamic) 'nothingness' that is neither some void nor *some* emptiness but, if any predication is permissable, the fullness or nothingness of pure intensity"

For the Gelugpa Prasangika, emptiness is never thought of metaphysically like this. For him, emptiness, even though he regards it as the ultimate nature of things, is dependently arisen. In other words, the only emptiness that can be known empirically is itself empty of inherent existence; it exists only in dependence on the impermanent things that are empty. For him, to understand this is more than sufficient to undo even the most subtle attachments, which allows him rest in the continual awareness of emptiness. In this way he avoids all karma which would result in rebirth in the ordinary world of Samsara. For him, karma or wilful action is the only creative principle that he knows of in this world, and he does not deign to ground it in an Absolute Being whose very nature is intrinsically unknowable. In relation to such a Being his position is agnostic.

The Shentongpa disagrees with the Gelugpa Prasangika on the nature of emptiness and correspondingly disputes the authenticity of his interpretation of the Prasangika view. The Shentongpa's understanding of Prasangika is likewise disputed by the Gelugpa. In the Shentong view, the discovery that things are empty of own being means not just that they lack inherent existence but that *they* do not exist at all. What one is experiencing is entirely real but not what one thinks it is. The Shentongpa understands the irrefutable fact of things' appearances as the display of an indeterminate ground of Absolute Being, also known as Buddha Nature, Emptiness, the Element or Sunyata. His experience of things' impermanence leads beyond self-emptiness to the awareness of continuous change, the subject of which cannot be grasped conceptually. Instead he tries to approach it by identifying facets of experience such as openness, clarity and sensitivity, that, like emptiness of self, remain immediately present regardless of change. Buddha Nature is understood to be the true essence of experience, which, in the original Greek sense of the term, is the same as saying that the two are substantially identical.

To the Gelugpa Prasangika, the notion of emptiness being substantially existent, is anathema and has no place in Buddhist methodology. But to the Shentongpa, this is no more than to admit the Buddha's recognition of the unconditioned as an actual reality[1]. To him, the experience of continuous change can be understood as nothing other than the presence of a single indeterminate all-encompassing Being. Furthermore, being all-encompassing, it is the true nature of one's own mind, the true ground of one's own being, in which all of one's particular experiences arise. Thus one's ordinary experience is not other than Emptiness, understood as this Absolute ground of Being. The Shentongpa, therefore, trains himself to see ordinary experience as the ephemeral display of non-dual Mind, a form of meditation quite different to that practised by the Gelugpa Prasangika.

These distinctions notwithstanding, I do not believe there to be any necessary fundamental differences between Gelugpa Prasangikas and Kagyu Shentongpas. The differences, I think, are superficial. For the Gelugpas' recognition that all forms of ordinary experience are dependently arisen, even awareness of emptiness, has to be realised in order for knowledge of unconditioned reality

---

[1] The confusion is exacerbated by the common use of the word "substance" as a synonym for "material". The word originally meant something akin to "objectively real".

to arise. Shentongpas who fail to understand this understand neither ordinary reality nor the unconditioned. On the other hand, any denial by Gelugpas that the unconditioned is a self-existent reality, is surely a perverse imposition of conditionality on the unconditioned. Why use the term if it cannot mean precisely what it purports to mean? A reality which is unconditioned is nothing other than a self-existent one. The two terms are synonymous. Thus, the Gelugpa's agnosticism in this regard is misplaced and unnecessary.

Some have maintained that the Shentongpas' view of self-existent Being (or energy) as the true nature of things, is theistic. This charge certainly merits examination. For clearly, the principle of dependence on ordinary causes and conditions is not regarded as sufficient by Shentongpas to account for the actuality of things. To the Shentongpa, that line of thinking leads to an infinite regression which ultimately accounts for nothing. Causes and conditions undoubtedly account for the particular nature of things but not for their immediate presence. How can they? They no longer exist? What the Shentongpa realises is that something real and continuous, which is not identical with ordinary things, is the true basis of their actuality. It is that reality that itself is the basis of their wilful actions. But since the Shentongpa is committed to the Buddhist view of conditioned existence as a state of suffering arisen from ignorant self-clinging, he must posit a basis for that self-clinging which does not in itself intend it. He surmounts this problem with the notions of spontaneity and mandala principle. Pure spontaneity is simply indeterminate creativity. And mandala principle is a general law of self-formation to which all created entities must conform. Beyond these general creative principles, the individual karma of creatures accounts for the eventual evolution of particular worlds. If anything, then, this a Deist view, similar to that held by Newton. The Absolute starts things off but then leaves them to themselves.

But now we are at an end of comparing Buddhist views of the unconditioned and are returning back to the book's main theme of the superiority of Christianity's revelation of a Trinitarian creator God, over Buddhism's self-creating universe.

Appendix B

(The following was originally prepared as a contribution to The Saint Austin Review under the title "A Return to Biblical Creationism".)

I am here going to put forward an argument which will try to reconcile the Aristotelian notion of substance with ways of thinking, such as the Buddhist notion of non-self, which usually lead to monistic or pantheistic conclusions. I do so without any pretensions of formal learnedness. I speak only as someone enthralled by the mystery of existence, with a wish to communicate his experience to others. Where I have erred in my understanding I welcome the correction of those who know better than myself.

The essence of the view of Genesis is captured very simply in the Bible's opening statement:

"In the beginning God created the heaven and the earth. The earth was without form and void, and darkness was upon the face of the deep; and the Spirit of God was moving over the face of the waters. And God said, 'Let there be light'; and there was light."

These are the fundamental acts of creation described in the first of the Bible's creation accounts, and are quite distinct from God's subsequent command that the earth and the waters bring forth living things. In the beginning, then, God creates something concrete and determinate, namely heaven and earth. These things may be "without form and void" in the sense that they do not as yet constitute a universe, but they are nevertheless heaven and earth, and are determinate to that extent. This is an important point.

For the entire conundrum of change which commanded so much attention from the philosophically minded, both in the East and in the West, was, according to the Bible, present in that first act of creation.

So what is the problem of change that philosophers were so transfixed by? It is simply this: if a thing changes, how can it remain the same thing? The simplicity of the question tends to conceal its profundity. Mostly, we take change for granted, unaware of any need to ask the question. Many people, however, *have* asked the question and come up with different answers. I am going to consider only two, Aristotle and the Buddha, Siddhartha Gotama.

Aristotle believed that only some continuous substantial principle capable of transmuting its form could account for things retaining their identity whilst changing. He believed this principle to be an inherent substratum which, along with form, substantiated things. This principle, which he called *primary matter*, was not absolutely identical with things since it existed in a perpetual state of flux. The matter of any given state is necessarily transmuted into other states with the passage of time. The continuity of a thing's form is preserved by the unity of primary matter, which ensures, as long as formal causes permit it, a continuous flow of matter through the thing. In other words, the continuity of primary matter, subject to the coherence of a thing's causes, ensures its enduring presence. Its changing being exists continuously, not as a series of unconnected states. Any thing, then, is a participant in a self-other relationship, the whole of which is substantiated by a single universal primary matter. Incidentally, no thing can be adequately defined in isolation from the self-other relationship to which it belongs, an insight which is the basis of an authentic though not absolute relativism.

Now, before going further we must acknowledge two different but related problems: those inherent in Aristotle's view; and those brought about by common misunderstandings of it. Most people understand the term "matter" as an element of common sense and assume that Aristotle is referring to that common sense notion of it. But in fact the common usage of the term, though useful, is superficial. It simply acknowledges the stuff of experience, the physical reality of things, a view which sees matter as something static, something which just exists. Aristotle's notion, in contrast, is evidently far more subtle. For though most of us have little difficulty in conceiving of universal matter, the realisation that this matter can have no separate existence of its own rarely occurs to us. It means that we are not talking about atoms, sub-atomic particles or even the energy fields popularly spoken of today. Though it only exists in particular formal states, primary matter's indeterminate nature means that its identity with those states is coincidental rather than absolute. It moves rather than resides within them. To reveal its existence is to reveal the true nature of things in their material aspect rather than the existence of a separate underlying reality. Materiality is recognised as something shared by all things. It is part of their nature and they, in their transmutability are revelations of its nature. In other words, things fundamentally are, in their materiality, primary material. They are not made out of it in the sense that *they* are merely illusory phenomena while *it* is true reality. Rather, they *are* it. It is the same as saying that, materially, there is but one world of primary matter, and all the different things are permutations or transmutations of that matter.

But matter, in this view, is entirely passive and cannot act. So what makes it move? Empirically, matter is already in movement and so generally movements can be traced back in a succession of causal events. This train of thought, however, leads to the notion of a prime mover, which, in being an uncaused cause, can only be God. Thus we arrive at the understanding that God created primary material and gave it motion when he created its first formal state, namely, the bi-polarity of heaven and earth.

It seems to me that the notion of an indeterminate material principle, helpful though it may appear to be to the problem of change, is a conceptual error. For me, it is axiomatic that materiality is, by its very nature, determinate. The material principle and primary matter, then, cannot be synonymous with each other. My argument is that we return to the simplicity of the biblical view: primary matter is "heaven and earth", not the material principle inherent in them. In this respect at least, I remain a Buddhist. Anything which is material has determinate form. It's nature, therefore, is conditioned and empty of self. What did the Buddha mean by this?

The Buddha, in the manner of his Indian culture, approached the problem of change differently to Aristotle.

His method might be described as a praxis of subjective analytical empiricism. It spurned all forms of speculation and hypothesis. The Buddha analysed his own being in a journey of discovery. His conclusions were not opinions but mere descriptions of his journey's destination and wayside stopping points. It is unsurprising, then, that his method led to quite different results to those of Aristotle. For though the Buddha recognised the unity and interdependence of conditioned things, he did not hypothesise the existence of an indeterminate universal *material* to account for the reality of things, but rather, what he named and described as the *unconditioned*. With regard to material and mental phenomena, he regarded both as dependently arisen and belonging to the domain of conditioned existence. He saw ignorant self-clinging as the primary cause of conditioned existence. What remained, when all clinging to existence had been overcome was the unconditioned, which in itself, was necessarily indeterminate.

On the question of the indeterminacy of primary matter, I believe the Bible to be supportive of the Buddha's view and regard his analysis of "heaven and earth", in this respect at least, as superior to Aristotle's. If I may cut to the chase, I believe that what we are searching for here is not a material principle in things, but a *materialising* principle. And that materialising principle is God's creative will. It is this Divine materialising principle that creates heaven and earth as an extensive continuum of determinate space and time, and causes it to form a universe which contains our world and its living creatures. There is no absolutely "real" stuff out of which things are made. Substantially, we are not made out of anything. We exist as immediate states of heaven and earth which is held in existence, that is to say, materialised, by God. Heaven and earth are determinate acts of God. That is what they *are*. And God is their sole *reifying* principle. He alone makes them real, not some material substance.

Thus, when Aristotle said that a thing's substance was the unity of its form and primary material, he was, in his own terms, wrong. That statement would only be true if primary material were regarded as heaven and earth. It ceases to be true when primary material is considered to be an indeterminate material principle. For there is no such principle, only a Divine substantiating, that is to say, creative, activity. And it is that which unites with a thing's form to give it its own individual substance.

Now, the reader may well be beginning to hear alarm bells ringing. Surely, if God is the sole reifying or substantiating principle in things, that amounts to nothing less than pantheism? I think not, and my answer to this question is, for me, a satisfactory clarification of just what it is in monistic and pantheistic systems of thought that should be rejected. At least in respect of actual substance, Aristotle's moderate realism set against the absolute realisms of his predecessors, and of the Buddha too, had it right. For by recognising the substantiality of the individual entity he accepted the essential propriety of things, that is to say, he accepted the givenness of their created natures and did not treat them as mere phenomena or illusory manifestations of some absolute reality.

For Buddhists, the true nature of reality is the unconditioned, what later became known by some as Buddha Nature. Worldly things, in contrast, were seen to be empty of self. For Aristotle, the true nature of things *was* their created worldly nature, and was quite distinct from either the prime mover or the primary material. His acceptance of thing's natures was not an act of reason. It was an act of faith. He had faith in his natural values as something empirically given, and thus conducted his philosophy as an active participant in reality, rather than pretending to be an otiose observer as Descartes recommended. His principle mistake, I believe, was in seeking to differentiate creatures from God by way of his indeterminate substantiating principle – primary matter.

For me, a thing's individual substance is real, not because of the unity of a real form and an indeterminate but real primary matter, but rather, because it is the real *meaning* of an act of God. Its separate reality lies in its God-given meaning. In other words, things do not convey meaning because they are objectively, substantially real. They are objectively and substantially real because that is the meaning conveyed by the acts of God which create them. Indeed, the continual Divine conveyance of that worldly meaning is none other than their creation as things which are real to themselves and to others. Only God, not substance or matter or form, or any combination of these, is able to reify things. The composite nature of the complex entities which make up our universe, indicates only an evolution of formal states of the true primary material held in existence by God – determinate heaven and earth. It is that Divine *holding-in-existence* of determinate matter that seems to me to provide the elusive indeterminate constant that Aristotle was searching for in his solution to the problem of change.

Crucifixion scene depicting Christ's agony

Bibliography

Principles of mainstream Buddhism:

"Dependent Origination"
  PA Payutto, Buddhadhamma, Found., 1994
"Good, Evil and Beyond"
  PA Payutto, Buddhadhamma Found., 1993
"What the Buddha Taught"
  Walpola Rahula, Wisdom, 1990
"Abhidharma in Daily Life"
  Nina Van Gorken, Triple Gem Press, 1994
"Buddhist Ethics"
  Hammalawa Saddhatissa, Wisdom, 1997

Original sources of mainstream Buddhism:

"Discourses of Gatama Buddha: Middle Collection"
  trans. D W Evans, Janus, 1992
"The Long Discourses of the Buddha: The Digha Nikaya
trans. Maurice Walshe, Wisdom, 1995

Studies of Buddhist teaching and history:

"Mahayana Buddhism"
  Paul Williams, Routledge, 1989
"Buddhism and Asian History"
  Kittagawa/Cummings, MacMillan, 1987
"The Buddha Within"
  Shenpen Hookham, SUNY, 1991

"Madhyamika and Yogachara"
Gadjin Nagao, SUNY, 1991
"Path to the Middle"
Kensur Yeshe Tupden/Anne C Klein, SUNY, 1994
"Natural Great Perfection"
Nyoshul Khenpo, Snow Lion, 1995
"A History of Buddhist Philosophy"
David Kalupahana, University of Hawaii, 1992

Original Sources of Mahayana Buddhism:

"Path of Heroes "
Zhechen Gyaltsab/Padma Gyurmed Namgyal,
Dharma, 1995
"Wisdom of Buddha: The Samdhinirmocana Sutra
publ. Dharma, 1995
"Master of Wisdom: Writings of the Buddhist Master
Nagarjuna"
trans. Chr. Lindtner, Dharma, 1986
"The Practice of Dzogchen"
Longchen Rabjam, Snow Lion, 1993

Principles of Catholicism:

"Apologetics and Catholic Doctrine"
Michael Sheehan, The Saint Austin Press, 2001
"Christianity"
D A Jones OP, Family, 1999
"A Catechism of Christian Doctrine"
Catholic Truth Society, 1997

"I Believe: A Little Catechism"
   Aid to the Church in Need, 1998
"A New American Catechism"
   Catholic Book Publishing Co., 1985
"The Catechism of the Catholic Church"
   publ. Geoffrey Chapman, 1994
"Crossing the Threshold of Hope"
   Pope John Paul II, Jonathan Cape, 1994
"Fundamentals of Catholic Dogma"
   Ludwig Ott, TAN, 1974
"Dogmatic Theology for the Laity"
   Rev. Matthias Premm, TAN, 1977
"A Tour of the Summa"
   Msgnr. Paul Glenn, TAN, 1978
      (Thomas Aquinas)
"Fundamentals of the Catholic Church"
   Peter Kreeft, Ignatius
"Catholicism: Christ and the Common Destiny of Man"
Henri de Lubac, Ignatius, 1988
"The Nature and Mission of Theology"
   Joseph Cardinal Ratzinger, Ignatius, 1995
"The Spirit of the Liturgy"
   Joseph Cardinal Ratzinger, Ignatius, 2000
"Dominus Iesus"
   Congregation for the Doctrine of the Faith, CTS, 2000

Catholic Bibles:

"The Holy Bible: Knox Version"
   Ronald Knox, Burns and Oates, 1955
"The Holy Bible: RSV Catholic Edition"
   publ. Ignatius

"The New Jerusalem Bible
publ. Darton, Longman and Todd, 1985
Standard Edition"

Papal Encyclicals:

"On Human Life"
Pope Paul VI, CTS, 1968
"Familiaris Consortio:The Christian Family in the
Modern World"
Pope John Paul II, CTS, 19881
"The Gospel of Life"
Pope John Paul II, Mediaspaul, 1995
"Salvifici Doloris: On Suffering"
Pope John Paul II, CTS, 1984
"Veritatis Splendor: The Splendour of Truth"
Pope John Paul II, CTS, 1993
"Fides et Ratio: Faith and Reason"
Pope John Paul II, CTS, 1998

Studies relating to East/West distinction:

"In the Beginning"
Joseph Cardinal Ratzinger, T&T Clark, 1990
"Word and Silence"
Raymond Gawronski SJ, T&T Clark, 1995
"The Invisible Father"
Louis Bouyer, T&T Clark, 1999
"Godfaring"
Francis Clark, St Pauls, 2000

Studies relating to gender differences:

"The Authority of Women in the Catholic Church"
Monica Migliorino Miller, Crisis Books, 1997

"The Church in the Culture War"
Joyce Little, Ignatius, 1995
"Prodigal Daughters"
ed. Donna Steichen, Ignatius, 1999
"Iron John"
Robert Bly, Element, 1990
"The Sibling Society"
Robert Bly, Penguin, 1997

Christian apologetics and studies of interest:

"God, Religion and Reality"
Stephen R L Clark, SPCK, 1998
"The Problem of Pain"
CS Lewis
"Elucidations"
Hans Urs Von Balthasar, Ignatius, 1998
"Love's Sacred Order"
Erasmo Leiva-Merikakis, Ignatius, 2000
"Meeting Other Believers"
Cardinal Francis Arinze, Gracewing, 1997
"Love is Stronger than Death"
Peter Kreeft, Ignatius, 1992
"Physics and the Ultimate Significance of Time"
ed. David R Griffin, SUNY, 1986
"Science and Evidence for Design in the Universe"
Behe, Dembski and Meyer, Ignatius, 2000